Gilly the Giraffe
Self-Esteem Activity Book

Gilly the Giraffe

Self-Esteem Activity Book

A Therapeutic Story with Creative Activities for Children Aged 5-10

Dr. Karen Treisman

Illustrated by Sarah Peacock

Jessica Kingsley *Publishers*
London and Philadelphia

First published in 2019
by Jessica Kingsley Publishers
73 Collier Street
London N1 9BE, UK
and
400 Market Street, Suite 400
Philadelphia, PA 19106, USA

www.jkp.com

Copyright © Karen Treisman 2019
Illustrations copyright © Sarah Peacock 2019

Library of Congress Cataloging in Publication Data
A CIP catalog record for this book is available from the Library of Congress

British Library Cataloguing in Publication Data
A CIP catalogue record for this book is available from the British Library

ISBN 978 1 78592 552 8
eISBN 978 1 78775 003 6

Printed and bound in Estonia

For Gill, a special, creative, and one-of-a-kind person – you are so missed, remembered, and loved.

Contents

About this Workbook

Hello, my name is Karen. I am a clinical psychologist, and I am also the author of this workbook, alongside the wonderful, colourful, creative, and helpful Gilly the Giraffe. The ideas in this workbook have helped lots of other children strengthen and build their self-esteem and confidence. This workbook is here to help you to:

- notice all of the things that make you special, unique, and cool
- give you lots of ideas for positive thinking and for celebrating the things that are going well
- build and strengthen your self-esteem, confidence, and self-belief.

What is inside this workbook

- First, there is the story of Gilly the Giraffe.
- Second, there are lots of fun activities for you to do around Gilly the Giraffe, such as a colouring-in page, a word search, a quiz, and some Gilly-inspired arts and crafts.
- Third, there are loads of different activities for you to do which help you strengthen, celebrate, notice, and build on your self-esteem, confidence, positive thinking, and self-belief.
- There is also a certificate at the end to celebrate you completing this workbook!

- After this, there is a whole section for the adult supporting you with this workbook to read, to give them lots more ideas to help you. They will need to read their part *first*, so that they can help you along the way.

Things to remember when reading this workbook

- Take your time – there is no rush – you can do a little bit at a time.
- The adults reading the workbook with you are there to help you along the way.
- Different activities and ideas will work and fit differently. So, you and the adult helping you can choose which ideas and activities you want to try.
- The most important bit is that you enjoy it.

Positive vibes and have fun!

From Karen and Gilly

The Story of
Gilly
the
Giraffe

Gilly the Giraffe lived in the African savannah, in the middle of the beautiful Ngorongora Crater in Tanzania, in East Africa.

She spent her days roaming gracefully through the vast grassy plains.

Although Gilly the Giraffe had many happy and wonderful things in her world, she still sometimes **felt worried, sad,** and that she just **wasn't good enough.**

Sometimes she felt as if she was different, and worse than the other animals.

Sometimes we all feel like that.

Gilly felt bad about herself because she was much taller than everyone else, which made her stand out from the crowd.

The flamingos gracefully sipped water while balancing on one leg, but she had to stretch her neck and bend her neck and legs to drink from the water hole. Gilly felt the other animals thought she looked silly.

Gilly's tongue was not pink like most other animals — it was long and black, which helped her to eat leaves from tall trees, but at the water hole she felt embarrassed using her tongue to lap up the cool water.

Finally, Gilly stood out because of the colourful mosaic patches that covered her whole body.

Gilly the Giraffe had some fantastic friends but some of the animals who didn't know her well would be unkind to Gilly. They would laugh, point, stare, and say mean things about her.

'Oh Gilly, you are so **uncool** with those **long legs!**'

'**Ha ha!** Look at her ugly **black tongue!**'

On days when Gilly the Giraffe felt sad and bad about herself, she would look at her reflection glistening in the water. She would wish that she was someone else – **anyone but Gilly!**

Gilly wanted to be liked by everyone. She really wanted to fit in and be just like all the other animals.

So, she would try to...

...make herself **shorter** by crouching down and stooping her head

...camouflage herself by colouring her patches in with mud

...use her gymnastic skills to find new ways of drinking from the water hole.

But whatever she tried, it didn't work – she was still Gilly the Giraffe!

One day, Gilly the Giraffe was feeling sad and was trying to hide from all the other animals behind the large green leaves of an acacia tree when she was spotted by **Loren the Lioness.**

She gruffly greeted Gilly, 'Peek-a-boo I found you.'

Gilly sighed and let out a snort, 'Of course you did! **I'm pretty hard to miss!'**

Loren grinned and said, 'That's true! Lucky you! That's what's great and special about you.'

Gilly the Giraffe looked surprised and confused. 'What do you mean that is what is special and great about me?'

Loren the Lioness let out a delighted roar. '**I love that you're different** – you're one of a kind. You bring colour and fun into the greenness of the trees, and you can reach the trickiest leaves with your long neck and tongue! Also, you are so kind and caring to everyone else!'

Loren pointed her paw. 'You remind me of a beautiful mosaic or patchwork, like the one on the sacred magical baobab tree over there!'

'That baobab tree is made up of many many different pieces. Some areas of the tree are smooth, some are rough, some are soft, some are big, some are small, and some are even fluffy; but when you put them all together, they fit like an amazing puzzle, and tell a wonderful story.

'Just like a rainbow, each colour is as important as the next. A rainbow would not look as magical if there was a colour missing.

'Imagine, a rainbow with no yellow, or no blue!'

Gilly the Giraffe strode up to the nearby mosaic baobab tree to take a closer look. She had never noticed how beautiful it was before, but could now see it clearly. She smiled. 'Wow, it really is a patchwork of colourful and beautiful pieces.'

Loren the Lioness nodded. 'And do you know what is **even more exciting**? Everyone who looks at the baobab tree will notice different patterns — it's just like looking through a kaleidoscope.'

Loren carried on, 'Sometimes, to truly
appreciate something and understand it
you need to **look at it in a new way.**

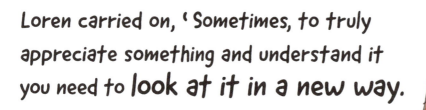

' Like...taking a really close
look with a magnifying glass. Or looking
at it from a great distance, as if you
were an eagle soaring high in the sky, or
had a magical carpet that could fly!'

Gilly the Giraffe looked excited. She started moving around the baobab tree, thinking about how she could discover a new way of looking at it.

She tried...

...pushing her face up close

...standing on her tippy toes to look down on it

...walking backwards until the baobab was so small and far away that it looked like a small shrub!

She was amazed. '**Wow**, you are right, Loren, it really does look different depending on how I look at it!'

Loren the Lioness nodded, agreeing: 'And it's not just the baobab tree. You see, Gilly, we are all different – no two animals are the same! That's what makes us all **special** and **cool**. We are all precious and deserve to be appreciated.'

Gilly the Giraffe smiled shyly. She had never thought of herself as special and cool! This was a whole new way of thinking about the world as well as looking at it – a bit like a **magic mirror**. She was still getting used to the idea, but did like the sound of it!

Gilly the Giraffe began thinking about what made her special.

'I suppose I quite like how I can make Halo the Hippo **laugh**...

'I'm quite **good at painting** with mud...

'I also have super sharp eyes. I can see almost the **whole savannah!'**

25

Loren the Lioness roared with laughter. 'You see? There are so many things that make you special — in fact, I bet you could fill a whole **treasure box** with the things that make you feel **good** and **special**.

'Maybe you could ask some of the other animals to see what ideas they have?'

The next day when Gilly arrived at Acacia Academy she cautiously approached her teacher Mrs Tengeru the Tortoise, and said, 'I know this might sound a bit strange but Loren the Lioness has been teaching me about how sometimes I forget the good things about me.

'I'd like to find out if there are things that you and my classmates at school like and appreciate about me. Could you help?'

Mrs Tengeru the Tortoise grinned. 'That's a great idea; let me have a moment to think...'

Gilly felt nervous while Mrs Tengeru quietly thought hard about Gilly and her **strengths.**

After some time, Mrs Tengeru spoke up, 'Well, Gilly, I've been thinking hard about your question, and I have a long list of things that are special about you!

'Two of my favourite things are that you have brilliant listening skills, and you're a very hard worker — especially in gymnastics!'

Gilly was surprised and proud to hear about these **positive treasures** from Mrs Tengeru.

Some of Gilly's classmates heard what Mrs Tengeru was saying and piped up.

'I can think of more! You're a great **peacemaker**! You're very **thoughtful** and always help to **calm** me when I'm arguing with someone!' exclaimed Zane the Zebra.

'You're the **best** classmate to have as a look-out and protect us from predators because of your **amazing** height!' chirped Oli the Oxpecker.

'You are really **friendly**, and **fun!**' shrieked Binnie the Baboon.

Wally the Warthog trotted over and rested a hoof on Gilly and snorted, 'I really like how your patches brighten up the savannah, like the sun.'

He continued, 'It's strange, but sometimes the things that you don't like about yourself are in fact your most **precious jewels.**

'Some animals used to be mean and horrible about my pig-like snout, but then I realised that it makes me unique: it helps me be a super-skilled digger, which makes me very useful indeed when a hole is needed!'

Mrs Tenguru was so excited by her class's team spirit and by how many ideas they were coming up with that she wrote down everyone's ideas on a tree trunk.

Binnie the Baboon chattered, 'It's **great to have a list** like this — it's just like keeping memories in your heart or in your head, but you can can look at the tree trunk and remember all those special things whenever you want to — especially if you can't remember them and are having a tricky day!'

Mrs Tengeru was very pleased with her tree trunk, but then she had another great idea. 'I know, why don't we play a game and think of lots of lovely words which match the letters of Gilly's name? When you do this, it's called creating an **acronym.**'

like the sun
peacemaker

friendly
watchtower
gymnastics

'How about G?' Mrs Tengeru asked.

'Ooh, definitely *generous*. Gilly always shares her favourite leaves with everyone,' Halo the Hippo croaked.

'I?' The classroom choir cheered in unison, '*Intelligent* and *interesting!*'

'L?' Binnie the Baboon excitedly barked, 'She is *loveable* and brings *loads* of *laughter* to us all!'

'Hmm...this is tricky, there is another L – any other ideas?' asked Mrs Tengeru.

'She's *loyal* – she has been a very good friend for a long time and is always there for me,' Zane the Zebra proudly shared.

'Wow! So many terrific things. Last, but not least, Y?'

'That's a difficult letter!' the class squealed.

'Ooh, I know,' said Wally the Warthog, 'How about *youthful*? She is so energetic and full of life!'

Mrs Tengeru clapped and cheered. 'What a great game, let's do this tomorrow for each of you! Everyone has things that make them special. We just need to notice, share, and celebrate them.'

Gilly was amazed at all of the new things that she was learning about herself.

'Maybe being **different is not so bad** after all. It might even be cool!'

GILLY
Generous
Interesting
Loveable
Loyal
Youthful

Later that day, Gilly reread all of the words on the tree trunk and used them to inspire one of her famous mud paintings.

It included all of the things that she was **proud** of, and that made her **special** and **happy**.

After finishing her mud painting, Gilly the Giraffe walked proudly out of Acacia Academy school. She was standing tall, with her head held high and her eyes sparkling brightly, and she walked with a spring in her step.

The sun bounced off her colourful **one-of-a-kind** mosaic of patches, creating beautiful rainbows across the savannah.

Activities

Introduction to the activities

This section features exercises and activities to help further explore the ideas covered in the story of Gilly the Giraffe.

Before carrying out any of the exercises with your child, please first read the Guide for Adults (pages 103–134) to familiarise yourself with the ideas that lie behind the activities, and how they can help your child. It features at the back of the book so that it does not get in the child's way.

You and your child will get much more out of the activities if you first have a good understanding of what they are doing and how they work.

What is next?

First, there are some fun activities, arts and crafts ideas, and quizzes for your child – do have fun and enjoy these!

Later activities (10–31) are designed to support your child to notice and celebrate their strengths, positive qualities, and special skills. There are also some ideas for how to remember and make special moments and memories even bigger.

Next, there are ideas for working with negative feelings and thoughts and for supporting children who have been subject to bullying or teasing (activities 33–34).

Finally, there are activities to encourage the child to reflect on their wishes and dreams for the future (36), and a certificate at the end for completing this book!

Part 1
Fun Activities and Crafts with Gilly

Gilly the Giraffe Colouring In

I hope you enjoyed reading the story of Gilly the Giraffe, and how she and her friends discovered that we all are special, unique, and cool in our own ways!

Activity 2
Gilly the Giraffe Word Search

Can you find all the words listed in the grid below?

```
R  S  B  X  A  O  O  V  G  Z  Q  Q  Z  X  T
I  S  G  O  K  P  B  F  H  Q  R  K  J  F  O
A  C  R  A  T  E  R  C  Q  L  T  C  Y  C  S
L  O  V  E  A  B  L  E  R  A  E  W  U  D  S
V  V  S  I  U  Z  C  N  J  K  K  N  D  F  S
F  Z  T  Y  G  C  U  I  O  D  J  N  N  W  B
G  J  J  A  C  R  O  N  Y  M  A  E  L  Y  B
L  N  O  X  P  I  Q  O  I  W  B  V  T  V  N
M  S  B  E  G  X  U  A  Y  Q  A  C  E  Y  Y
C  N  Q  A  F  I  Y  K  C  K  U  Z  H  S  B
Z  P  R  D  O  G  R  S  P  A  I  E  K  D  U
R  K  D  I  M  B  I  A  G  C  C  I  L  Q  L
L  E  L  I  O  N  A  L  F  P  O  I  S  G  I
E  C  H  J  H  N  I  B  L  F  I  O  A  U  K
R  L  S  P  E  C  I  A  L  Y  E  P  L  M  Y
```

GILLY	UNIQUE	LION
GIRAFFE	SPECIAL	CRATER
BAOBAB	COOL	ACACIA
ACRONYM	LENNY	LOVEABLE

Quiz and Questions about Gilly the Giraffe and about What Is Cool about Being Yourself!

1. Where in the world does Gilly live?
2. What different colours are Gilly's patches?
3. Why does Gilly feel different?
4. What did Gilly do to try to be like everyone else, and to fit in?
5. Where does Gilly try to hide?
6. What colour is Gilly's tongue?
7. What is the lioness's name in the story?
8. What makes Wally the Warthog special and different?
9. What is the name of Gilly's teacher?
10. What type of tree is in the book?
11. Where does Mrs Tengeru write down all of the great ideas?
12. What game did they play at school to help think of all of the positive things about Gilly?
13. What things does Gilly learn she is really good at?
14. Who are some of Gilly's friends and helpers?

Answers

1. In the middle of the beautiful Ngorongora Crater in Tanzania, in East Africa.
2. Her patches are like a mosaic — red, blue, pink, green, orange, purple.
3. She is taller than the other giraffes, has a long, black tongue and her body is covered in colourful mosaic patches.
4. She would crouch down to make herself seem shorter, camouflage herself by covering her patches in mud, and use her gymnastic skills to find new ways to drink from the water hole.
5. She tries to hide behind the tall tree.
6. Black.
7. Loren.
8. His pig-like snout helps him to be a super-skilled digger.
9. Mrs Tengeru the Tortoise.
10. Baobab tree.
11. On a tree trunk.
12. They made an acronym by thinking of words to match the letters of Gilly's name.
13. She has brilliant listening skills, is a very hard worker, a great peacemaker she is friendly, thoughtful, and calm, protects her friends, and her mosaic patches brighten up the savannah.
14. Loren the Lioness, Zane the Zebra, Wally the Warthog, Oli the Oxpecker, Binnie the Baboon.

Activity 4

Some Extra Questions about the Story of Gilly and the Themes within the Story

Talk with the adult supporting you with this workbook about these questions.

1. Why do you think thinking and feeling good about ourselves is important?
2. What do you think happens when we feel and think negatively about ourselves?
3. What are some of the disadvantages of thinking negatively?

Talk with an adult about your thoughts. Try making a poster or drawing your ideas about negative thoughts. Next try answering these questions. Remember, there are no right or wrong answers!

1. What do you think the world would be like if we were all exactly the same?
2. How would you feel about living in that world?
3. What would be some of the disadvantages if everyone was the same?
4. What is cool about being different?

If you like, you can make a poster or draw your ideas about a world where everyone is the same! What is one thing (even if it is really tiny) that makes you different, and which you like?

Activity 5
Make Your Own Gilly the Giraffe!

Gilly can help you remember all of the things that make you special and cool. She can also remind you to be proud, confident, and to be *you*! These are just a few ideas for arts and crafts activities to create your own Gilly – you may have other great ideas!

Gilly the Giraffe using toilet rolls

Gilly head and neck

A simple creation that uses a kitchen roll cardboard tube and paper or card.

1. Use a long cardboard roll (kitchen roll size) to make Gilly's neck.
2. Colour it in and decorate the neck with Gilly's patches.
3. Cut out Gilly's head and ears using paper and decorate them with her eye, nose, mouth, ossicones (horns on her head), and ears.

Gilly whole body

This more ambitious model uses a kitchen roll cardboard tube and four smaller toilet roll tubes.

1. Use pens, pencils, crayons, or paints to colour the toilet roll for Gilly's neck (the kitchen roll) and body (one of the four toilet rolls) – you can copy Gilly's patterns or invent new ones of your own!
2. Pick up another toilet roll and draw on Gilly's eyes and mouth – this will be Gilly's head.
3. Use sticky tape to join the rolls together as you can see in the photo. The coloured-in kitchen roll is for Gilly's long neck, the coloured-in toilet roll her body, the roll with eyes and mouth her head, and the two blank rolls are for her two pairs of legs.
4. Cut out card or paper to create ear shapes, her rainbow mane, her ossicones (the horns on her head) and her tail, and stick these on too.

Gilly the Giraffe using a paper plate

To create Gilly's head, all you need is a paper plate, some paper or card, and some pencils or pens to colour in. You can also use goggly eyes, which you can buy in craft shops.

1. Take the paper plate and turn it around. Paint or colour the back of the plate as Gilly's face.
2. Draw on her eyes or use goggly eyes.
3. Cut out her ears and her ossicones using paper or card and colour them in.
4. Stick on the ears and ossicones using glue or sticky tape.

Gilly the Giraffe hand prints

Head and neck

Make your very own Gilly the Giraffe using just your hands!

1. For the first hand print creation, draw on a piece of paper around your hand and arm (or someone else's) as far as your elbow.
2. If you prefer, you could use some yellow ink or paint to make a hand print, and then draw the neck afterwards.
3. Colour in your hand outline and add Gilly's ossicones, her mane, her face, and her patches using a pen or pencil.

Whole body

1. For the second hand print craft of Gilly, draw around your hand (or someone else's), or create aa hand print using yellow ink or paint, but make sure to do it at the top of the page with some blank space beneath.
2. Turn your hand print around so the hand is at the bottom of the page with fingers pointing towards you — your fingers will be Gilly's legs, and your thumb will be Gilly's tail.
3. Now you can draw in Gilly's neck and face, and decorate her body!

Gilly the Giraffe finger puppet

1. Find a stiff piece of card that won't flop when you hold it up.
2. Draw the shape of Gilly (see the image for the shape to draw) and cut it out.
3. You can either do this as one drawing, or cut the head and body first, then stick on the ears and ossicones. You can even cut out the body, head and neck shapes separately, then glue or sticky tape them together.
4. Colour Gilly in using paints, pencils, pens, or crayons.
5. Ask an adult to help make two holes in the middle of Gilly's body big enough to fit your fingers into.
6. When you've finished the puppet, put your fingers in the holes and make Gilly walk around!

Activity 6

Me and the People in My Life – Animal Fun!

Draw or write answers to the questions below — or if you prefer, sculpt or make a creation using art materials! Use a different piece of paper if you need more space.

- Which animal is your favourite animal, and why? _____

_____

_____

_____

_____

_____

_____

- If you were an animal, which one would you be, and why? _____

_____

_____

_____

_____

_____

_____

- What would you look like?

_____

_____

_____

_____

_____

_____

- What would you sound like?

_____
_____
_____
_____
_____
_____
_____
_____

- How would you spend your time?

_____
_____
_____
_____
_____
_____
_____

- What animals would your friends, teachers, and family be, and why?

_____
_____
_____
_____
_____
_____

Me as a Superhero or Magical Creature

Imagine yourself as a superhero or as a magical creature and answer the questions below.

- What is your name? _____

- What do you look like? _____

  _____

  _____

- What do you sound like? _____

  _____

  _____

- What do you like to say? _____

  _____

  _____

- How do you spend your time? _____

  _____

  _____

- What superpowers do you have? _____

  _____

  _____

- Where do you live? _____

- How do you feel when you are the superhero or magical creature? ___

  _____

  _____

  _____

Now draw a picture of you as the superhero or magical creature! Use a blank sheet of paper if you need more space.

List of Positive Descriptors and Adjectives

These can be used to guide all of the strengths-based exercises discussed, or can be directly circled, underlined, or highlighted by the child, worker, or surrounding adults.

Able	Accepting	Accomplished	Active
Adaptable	Adorable	Adventurous	Affectionate
Agile	Alert	Amazing	Ambitious
Amusing	Analytical	Animated	Appreciative
Articulate	Artistic	Assertive	Attractive
Authentic	Aware	Awesome	Balanced
Blissful	Bold	Brave	Bright
Brilliant	Calm	Capable	Caring
Charming	Cheerful	Clean	Clear
Communicative	Compassionate	Competent	Connected
Conscientious	Considerate	Consistent	Content
Cool	Courageous	Creative	Cuddly
Cultured	Curious	Cute	Daring
Dazzling	Delightful	Dependable	Determined
Divine	Down-to-earth	Dreamy	Dynamic
Eager	Easy	Educated	Efficient
Elegant	Empathetic	Empowering	Enchanting
Energetic	Engaged	Enthusiastic	Ethical

Excellent	Excitable	Exciting	Explorative
Exquisite	Extraordinary	Fabulous	Fair
Faithful	Fantastic	Fashionable	Fearless
Feisty	Flexible	Focused	Forgiving
Forward-thinking	Friendly	Fun	Funky
Funny	Generous	Gentle	Genuine
Giving	Glamorous	Gorgeous	Graceful
Grand	Grateful	Great	Groovy
Grounded	Handsome	Happy	Hardworking
Helpful	Honest	Honourable	Hopeful
Humble	Idealistic	Imaginative	Incredible
Independent	Innovative	Inquisitive	Insightful
Inspiring	Interested	Interesting	Intuitive
Inventive	Jazzy	Jolly	Jovial
Joyous	Just	Keen	Kind
Knowledgeable	Light-hearted	Lively	Logical
Loveable	Lovely	Loving	Loyal
Lucky	Magical	Magnificent	Marvellous
Mature	Mellow	Mind-blowing	Motivated
Motivational	Musical	Natural	Neat
Nice	Noble	Nourishing	Nurturing
Open	Open-minded	Optimism	Organised
Original	Outgoing	Outstanding	Patient
Peaceful	Persevering	Phenomenal	Playful

Polite	Positive	Powerful	Practical
Precious	Pretty	Proactive	Problem-solver
Proud	Punctual	Purposeful	Quality
Quiet	Radiant	Real	Realistic
Reasoned	Reflective	Refreshing	Relaxed
Reliable	Resilient	Resourceful	Respectful
Rigorous	Risk-taking	Romantic	Secure
Sensible	Serene	Skilled	Smart
Smiley	Smooth	Sociable	Soothing
Sparkly	Spectacular	Spiritual	Splendid
Spontaneous	Sporty	Spunky/swag	Stable
Steady	Strong	Successful	Sunny
Super	Supportive	Surprising	Survivor
Sweet	Talented	Tender	Terrific
Thorough	Thoughtful	Timeless	Tolerant
Traditional	Tranquil	Transparent	Triumphant
Trooper	Trustworthy	Truthful	Unbelievable
Understanding	Unflappable	Unreal	Uplifting
Useful	Valuable	Versatile	Vibrant
Victorious	Virtuous	Vulnerable	Warm
Welcoming	Willing	Wise	Witty
Wonderful	Worthy	Youthful	Yummy
Zealous	Zesty		
What else?			

Activity 9
Create Your Own Acronym!

You can create your own acronym, just like Gilly the Giraffe! You can use your first, middle, or last name, or all of your names — or even your nickname!

1. Write the letters of your name down the left-hand side of a page, starting from the top-left-hand corner of a blank page (see examples).
2. Once you have written your name, try to think of a word that starts with the first letter you've written down. It needs to be a positive word — maybe something about you, your personality, your skills, or things that you are good at.
3. Move on to the next letter until you've reached the end of your name!

Once you've written down your ideas, try talking to other people to get even more words, just like Gilly did, and add these to your list.

Like Gilly, you can ask your friends, your teacher or other adults who know you very well. Ask them, 'What things do you love, appreciate, or admire about me?'

Sometimes, it can be difficult to think of positive words, especially when trying to match them to a particular letter.

To help you with this, have a look at Activity 8 which has lots of ideas and suggestions of positive words.

Once you've finished your acronym, create a picture, poster, or piece of art out of your name acronym. Here are some other fun things to do with your name:

- Make your name using items from nature or from different materials. You could try using stones, twigs, leaves, grass, flowers, feathers, pebbles, bark, pine cones, shells, conkers, buttons, stickers, glitter, pompoms, or feathers.

- Make your name using pasta pieces, rice, dry beans, lentils, or other dry foods.

- Think of objects that start with the letters of your name — for example, for the letter A, you could have an apple, ant, atlas, art, antelope, arrow, avocado, or arm!

- Think of things you like doing or seeing that go with the letter of your name — for example, B: bowling, ballet, bike, bathing, brushing my hair.

Part 2
Activities and Exercises for Strengthening My Self-Esteem, Confidence, Positive Thinking, and Self-Belief

Sentence Completion – Positives and Strengths!

Completing sentences is another thing we can do to help us to think about some of the positives and strengths in our lives.

Read the sentences below and have a go at finishing each sentence – write down, draw, or say your ending out loud. There are no right or wrong answers!

If you like, find people to help you answer them. You could just choose a few sentences to start with, or if you feel ready, go ahead and complete them all!

- Something I love about myself is... _____

_____

_____

- Something I am thankful and grateful for is... _____

_____

_____

- Something I do which makes other people happy is... _____

_____

_____

- Something that puts a smile on my face is... _____

_____

_____

- Something I can do well is... _____

_____

_____

- The best compliment I've ever received is... _____

_____

_____

- Something that makes me laugh is... _____

_____

_____

- My favourite thing about me is... _____

_____

_____

- I am proud of... _____

_____

_____

- I am confident when... _____

_____

_____

- I am excited about... _____

_____

_____

- A kind thing I have done is... _____

_____

_____

- Something that makes me unique is... _____

_____

_____

- I can teach other people how to ... _____

_____

_____

- I am happy when... _____

_____

_____

- I am lucky because... _____

_____

_____

- I surprised myself when... _____

_____

_____

- My favourite memory is... _____

_____

_____

- Something funny about me is... _____

_____

_____

- I admire... _____

_____

_____

- My favourite people are... _____

_____

_____

- My wish for myself is... _____

_____

_____

- My wish for other people is... _____

_____

_____

- My wish for the world is... _____

_____

_____

- The best time of my week is... _____

_____

_____

- My favourite thing to do is... _____

_____

_____

- I am strong because... _____

_____

_____

- I am special because... _____

_____

_____

- I am cool because... _____

_____

_____

- I'm at my best when I... _____

_____

_____

- A problem I have solved is... _____

_____

_____

- I would give myself an award for... _____

_____

_____

- I feel good about myself when... _____

_____

_____

- My dream is to... _____
_____
_____

- I have fun when... _____
_____
_____

- When I grow up I want to... _____
_____
_____

Extra activities!

There are other things you can do with your favourite sentence.

A girl called Maisie liked the sentence, 'When I grow up, I want to...' She wanted to work with horses and to have long hair. So, she made a beautiful painting of her looking much older, with long hair, and with horses. She also added things about the horses' names, and how she felt.

A boy called Jesse liked the sentence, 'I would give myself an award for...' He completed it by saying 'being a good big brother' and chose to make a collage of photos of him and his brother, then wrote a song as to why he liked being a big brother.

Can you choose your favourite sentence, and make a story, a play, a poem, a comic strip, or a piece of art? It could be a painting, a sign, a collage, or a poster!

Another idea could be to use the sentences to create a game — cut them out or write them on a piece of paper, then put them into a treasure chest (a bag or jar) or hide them and create a treasure hunt!

Activity 11
Positive Picture or Collage

Draw a positive picture or create a collage by sticking images or letters cut out from magazines, papers, and newspapers onto a piece of paper.
Write one of the sentences from Activity 10 — for example:

- I am proud of...

- My favourite memory is...

- My favourite thing about me is...

- I am happy when...

- My dream is to...

Or create your own positive sentence!

Activity 12
Positive Portrait

Draw or paint your best, happiest, most confident
self below.

You can also write all of the great things about you around the edges of
the mirror.

If you prefer, you can put a favourite photo of yourself in the middle
and write all of the good things about you around it.

Some of your answers to the sentences in Activity 10 might give you
some ideas.

Activity 13
Sentence Completion – All About Me

As we learned in the story of Gilly the Giraffe, each one of us is unique, cool, and special in our own way.

It is great to spend some time thinking about who we are, what we like, and what makes us special.

This can include thinking about the different parts of our selves. To get us started try completing these sentences. There are a lot, so just have a go at the ones you feel like. You can always finish the rest later.

- The things I love are... _____
_____
_____

- The things that makes me happy are... _____
_____
_____

- The things that make me laugh are... _____
_____
_____

- The things that make me cry are... _____
_____
_____

- The things I like to do are... *(think about your hobbies and interests)*
_____
_____

- My favourite place to visit is... _____
_____
_____

- My best friend is... _____

_____

_____

- My favourite colour is... _____

_____

_____

- My favourite food is... _____

_____

_____

- My best time of year is... _____

_____

_____

- My favourite movie or TV show is... _____

_____

_____

- My favourite book or story is... _____

_____

_____

- If I could wish anything it would be... _____

_____

_____

- If I could visit any place in the world I would visit... _____

_____

_____

- My favourite smell is... _____

_____

_____

- My favourite thing to touch is... _____
_____
_____

- My favourite animal is... _____
_____
_____

- My favourite fictional character or superhero is... _____
_____
_____

- My favourite sport is... _____
_____
_____

- My favourite song, singer, or band is... _____
_____
_____

- My favourite toy, item, or most precious possession is... _____
_____
_____

- Someone I admire is... _____
_____
_____

- My favourite memory or moment is... _____
_____
_____

What other favourites would you like to add? _____
_____
_____

Feelings

Now let's spend some time thinking about our feelings. Have a go at completing these sentences:

- The things that make me feel happy are... _____
  _____
  _____

- You know I am happy when I... _____
  _____
  _____

- The things that make me feel excited are... _____
  _____
  _____

- You know I'm excited when I... _____
  _____
  _____

What other feelings can you think of? What makes you feel like that? How can others tell when you feel like that?

_____
_____
_____
_____
_____
_____
_____
_____
_____
_____

Activity 14
Getting Creative – All About Me

Make a creation that shows who you are, what you like and all of the different parts of you — for example what you are like, what you are interested in, what you love and what you're great at — as well as the things you really don't like! If you've already done Activity 10, you could use that as a reminder.

Try to use all of your creativity and your imagination. You could create a collage, a poster for the wall, or a picture, or write a story — you could even try writing a poem!

If you have your own camera, or are allowed to borrow an adult's camera, try taking photos to capture your ideas and discoveries.

Here are some more cool ways to express who you are.

All About Me collage

Make an All About Me collage using magazines, images, pictures, photos, and materials.

You can also make an All About Me comic strip, scrapbook, poem, story, song, rap, poster, flag, shield, or sign!

All About Me Russian dolls

You could use blank Russian dolls (you can buy these at www.safehandsthinkingminds. co.uk), or instead draw some Russian dolls on a piece of paper, to show the different parts of your personality, your interests, hobbies, things that are important to you and things you are good at.

All About Me puzzle pieces

Add one positive thing about your personality, interests, or likes to each jigsaw puzzle piece then put them together to combine all the bits that make you! Cut pieces out, use a template (I've included one for Activity 18) or stick things on an actual floor puzzle.

You can do the same with separate bits of patchwork, which you could make out of different materials or coloured paper, just like the baobab tree — lots of different bits that make up a beautiful whole.

All About Me doll or puppet

Draw all of the different parts of your personality, skills, talents and interests on a blank doll, on a teddy, on masks, or on a puppet.

All About Me body outline

This needs a really big piece of paper, big enough for you to lie on!

Get someone to draw around your body, then write or draw the different things about you inside the outline of the body!

If you don't have a huge piece of paper, you can still draw an outline of yourself and draw in all the different parts of you. In this photo, someone has created a 'puzzle person' using the template from Activity 23.

All About Me LEGO® sculpture

Try showing all of the different parts of you on a Jenga® or LEGO® sculpture — drawing or sticking pieces of paper on to the different bricks (see also Activity 20).

All About Me hand

Draw around your hand, or do a hand print using ink or paint. Draw or write all the different parts of you on it. You can write these down or use materials, stickers, and pictures to decorate and bring them to life!

All About Me treasure box

Make an All About Me treasure box or container, just like Gilly's, and decorate the outside with pictures or materials which tell other people all about you. Fill the inside with items: writing on paper, souvenirs, or objects you value which say even more about you as a person.

All About Me object

Choose something you love and which makes you feel good and happy. Draw a picture of it, then write down all of the different parts of your personality and things about you either on it or around the edges of it.

You could create a rainbow or a shining sun — other ideas could be petals on a flower. It could even be planets in a galaxy, words on a globe, words on a heart, words on a train, or words on different parts of a superhero (see also Activity 22).

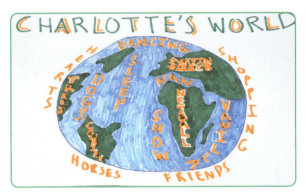

- **Which is your favourite idea?** _____
  _____
  _____

- **Which, if any, would you like to try?** _____
  _____
  _____

- **Do you have a different idea which you'd prefer to do?** _____
  _____
  _____

Self-Esteem and Sensory Hands

As Gilly learned, each one of us is wonderfully unique and different — that is what makes us all special and cool!

For example:

- Did you know that no two giraffes have the same patches?

- Did you also know that no two gorillas have the same nose?

- Did you know that no two people have the same hand prints?

Amazingly, we all have our very own, one of a kind, unique hands!

Self-esteem hand

For this activity:

1. Draw around your hand (or both hands!). If you prefer, you can make a hand print using ink or paint, or even just cut out the shape of a hand.
2. Then on each finger and thumb, write down:
    1. Something that I like about myself
    2. Something that other people like about me
    3. Something I am proud of
    4. Something that I enjoy doing
    5. Something that I am good at.

If you have done two hands, you can keep on adding more positive skills, talents, and qualities to your other fingers and thumb. You can also use some other categories from Activity 10.

Sensory hand

As well as a self-esteem hand, you can also create a *sensory hand*. On a sensory hand, you write the things that make you feel happy, relaxed, and calm but think about your five senses:

- Things I like to *smell*

- Things I like to *touch or feel*

- Things I like to *taste or eat*

- Things I like to *see*

- Things I like to *hear*.

All about Me hand

You can also do an All About Me hand (see Activity 14).

My hand!

Draw, write, or paint below your hand (or hands!)

Activity 16
Treasure Hunt

You may not know this, but it's a fact that the more we look for something and pay attention to it, the more it grows!

Think about a flower. The more you look after it — water it, give it good soil, maybe even talk to it! — the healthier it becomes and the taller and stronger it grows!

Think about a treasure hunt — the harder you look for the treasure, the more places you look, and the more time you spend looking for clues, the more likely it is that you will be able to find it!

This is important to remember, because we all have treasures inside us — we just need to learn how to find, notice, enjoy, and appreciate them. Our treasures can be positive things about us — our personality, our talents, our skills, things we can do, things we like, or things about us that people like.

Below are some ideas for carrying out your very own treasure hunt.

You can also design your own. There are lots to choose from, as we are all unique, so you can choose your favourite one/s to fill in, or you can come up with your own ideas — there is a treasure box, a patchwork, a peacock, a puzzle, a shield, a tower, a snowflake, a star, and a rainbow!

Ideas for an outdoor treasure hunt
Can you find or see:

- a green leaf
- a pine cone
- some brown bark
- some grass
- an insect
- a stick or twig
- a rock
- a flower
- a feather

- a bird
- a cloud
- something blue
- some mud
- a surprise?

Ideas for an indoor treasure hunt

Can you find or see:

- a book
- a blanket
- a teddy
- a shoe
- a pen or pencil
- a magazine or newspaper
- a spoon
- something round
- a tissue
- something shiny
- a hair brush
- something soft?

Activity 17
Treasure Box

Remember, it's a fact that the more we look for something and pay attention to it, the more it grows! We also have treasures *inside* us — we just need to learn how to find, notice, enjoy, and appreciate them. Our treasures can be positive things about us — our personality, our talents, our skills, things we can do, things we like, or things about us that people like.

What different treasures are inside you?

Write or draw your treasures on or around the treasure box below.

Patchwork of Positives and of My Personality

Fill in the positive personality patchwork below with all of your positive qualities, talents, skills, things you can do, things you like, and things about you that people like.

You can also colour it in or decorate it — whatever you'd like to do!

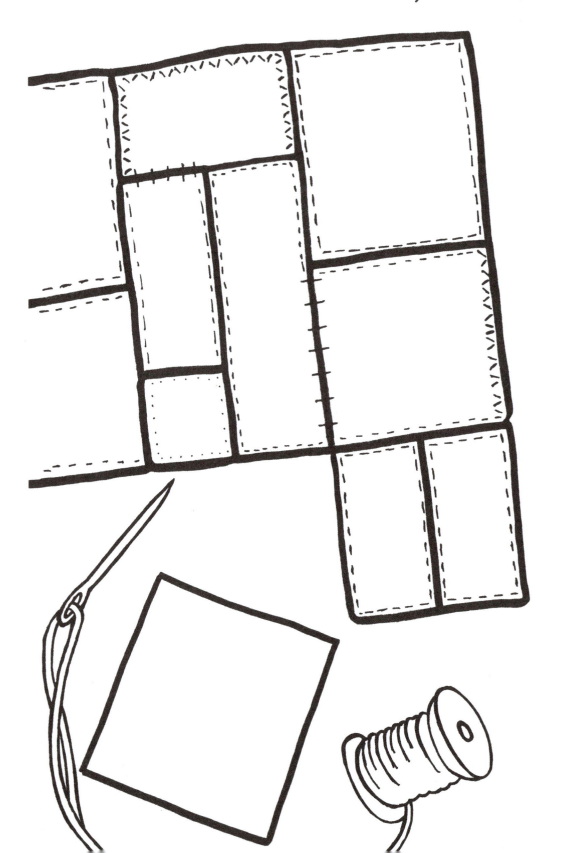

Every Snowflake Is Different

Every snowflake is different and special; no two snowflakes are the same. What are all the things that make you special and unique? Draw or write your answers.

Tower of Strengths or Skyscraper of Strengths

Write down or draw all of your strengths, positives, and skills on the different bricks. If you prefer, you can also do this using real blocks, for example with Jenga® or LEGO®. Your friends, helpers, and family can help you think of positives too!

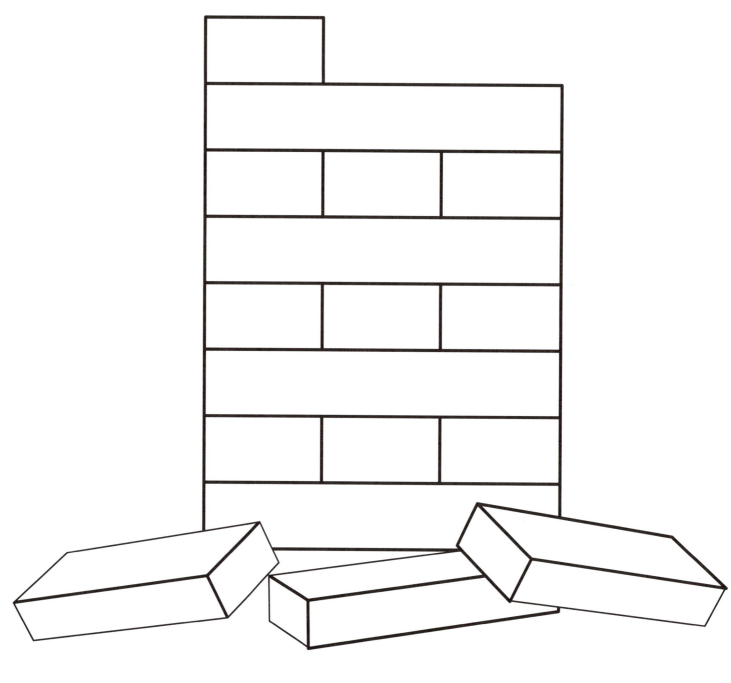

Positive Personality and Proud Peacock

Draw or write down the things that make you and the people you care about proud as peacocks!

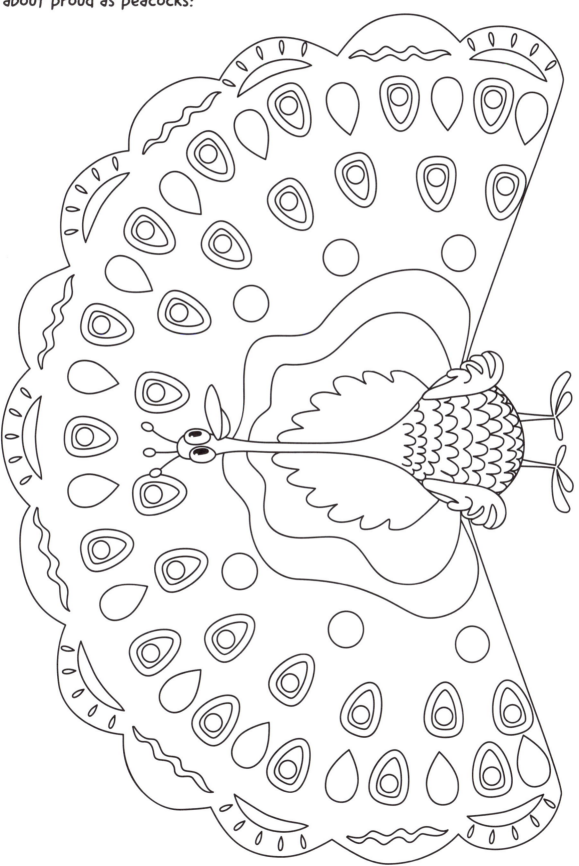

Activity 22
Rainbow of Resources

Write down or draw on the different rainbow stripes all your positive qualities, talents, resources, things you can do, things you like, and things about you that people like.

Positive Puzzle Person

Write down or draw on the different person puzzle pieces all of the positive things about you (see also Activity 14 for other ideas).

Activity 24
Award, Trophy, or Medal

If I were going to give myself an award, a trophy, or a medal it would be for...

Draw or write what it would be for on the award below. Imagine yourself being given and receiving this award! This might also be what award your friends, teachers, pets, or family would give you.

Activity 25
Strengths-Based Activities Extended

The ideas from Activities 17—24 which focus on strengths can be brought to life in pieces of art too — they don't just need to be on pieces of paper.

Here are some examples, and a few new ideas; however, be as creative and imaginative as you wish!

This is some of Lucy's strengths turned into beautiful and colourful awards (see Activity 24).

This is Tristan's Positive Patchwork using bright pieces of material (see Activity 18).

This is a treasure box filled up with different items, sticky notes, and pieces of gems which represent all of Marlie's strengths, skills, and positive qualities.

This is Skyla's Body of Brilliance. She has used a cut-out of a body, and written all of the things she loves and is good at on the body. She has also written what her body does, why it is useful, and how she can look after her body.

This is Astyn's Skyscraper of Strengths. Each strength, skill, and positive quality is written on a label and stuck on a piece/brick of LEGO®. You could use any building blocks or pillow for this (see Activity 20).

This is all of Georgia's strengths and skills written down around a star of strengths and skills. You could also do this around a shield, a sun, a rainbow, and so many more ideas!

Which, if any, of these ideas would you like to try, and do you think could be fun?

Activity 26
If I Ruled the World

Write or draw what your world would look like, feel like, and be like if you ruled the world. What rules would there be? Who would live there? What type of leader would you be?

Special Moments I Want to Remember and Keep Safe

Sometimes when we are feeling sad, scared, upset, frustrated, and so on, it is helpful to remember all of the special memories we have experienced.

Try to answer some of the following questions. Draw, write, talk about, sculpt, or mould your answers.

- What are some of your best and favourite times, moments, and memories? _____

_____

_____

_____

_____

_____

_____

_____

- What are some of the times you were happiest? _____

_____

_____

_____

_____

_____

_____

_____

_____

- What moment do you wish you could travel back to in a time machine?

....
....
....
....
....
....
....
....

- Which moment, if you could, would you play over and over again, like a film? ....
....
....
....
....
....
....

- Which memory or moment always makes you smile, feel good, and laugh?

....
....
....
....
....
....
....

There are lots of different ways we can try to remember these special times even more, and keep clear memories.

If you do this, you can look at them whenever you want or need to. They will always be with you in your heart, in your body, and in your mind.

Some of these ideas are shown on the next page. You might like to try a few of them, or you might have your own ideas!

The grown-up supporting you with this book can help you with these activities.

Window of happiness

Write or draw a special memory or moment which you want to keep remembering and revisiting in each pane of the window.

Chocolate box of happiness, memories, gifts, and moments

Fill a chocolate box up with all of the special, happy, sweet moments you have had in your in life.

Treasure box or memory box

Decorate and fill a box up with all of your treasured, happy, and positive moments, souvenirs, and memories. You can write or draw these on paper, or you can add memory items. You can also write down the memories on things like stars or hearts.

Journey jar

Write down all of your positive and happy moments and memories and add them to a jar, box, or container. Then whenever you need a little boost or reminder, you can open the jar up and read them. You can also look and see that the jar is full and bursting with special times and moments.

Positive magnet

You can write on or around a magnet all of the good, happy, and special things, words, advice, memories, and moments that you want to stick with you and remember. This can help power-up your positive magnet (see also Activity 28).

Time capsule

Make your very own time capsule and fill it with all the best things and memories you want to keep safe (or read Activity 29 and write these things down).

Bottled-up moments

Fill up or decorate bottles with the moments which you want to remember and hold on to (using items, sand, labels, etc.). See also Activity 30.

Sparkle diary, superhero moments diary, treasure box diary

Write down in a diary, scrapbook, or journal all of your special moments, experiences, and thoughts. These also can be filled in on your very own treasure box diary (see also Activity 31).

- Which are your favourite tricks and tools?
- Which ones do you want to try out?
- What other ideas do you have?

To build on the above, the Magnetic Moments, Time Capsule, and Bottle Up activities will follow.

Magnetic Moments, Memories, Thoughts, Feelings, and Sensations

Draw or write all of the wonderful, positive, supportive, happy moments, memories, thoughts, advice, feeling, and sensations you want to stick with you, and which you will use to power-up your positive magnet.

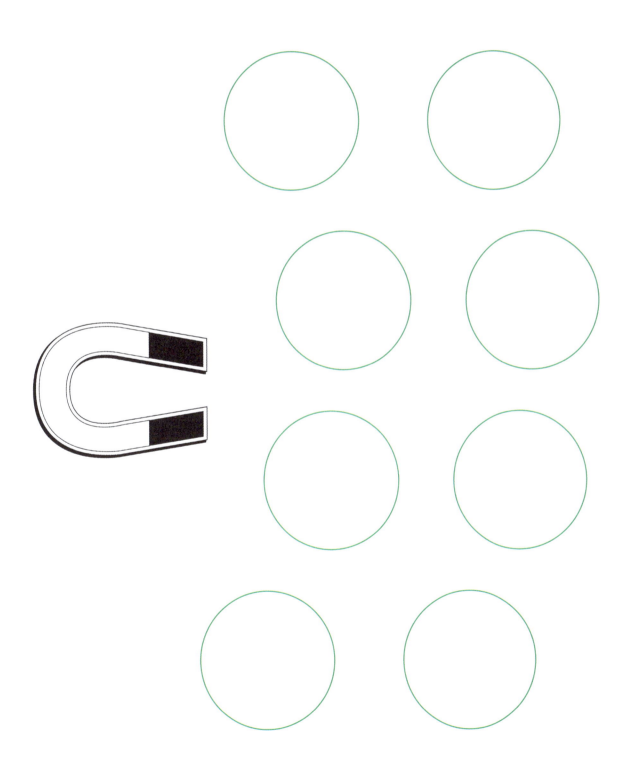

Time Capsule

Fill in the picture below, or make your very own time capsule and then fill it with all of the best things and memories you want to keep safe.

Activity 30
Bottle Up

This is like taking a photo in your mind, or truly soaking in a special moment. Which moments, memories, people, and times would you want to bottle up and why? Write or draw on the bottles below — try to give each one a label. If you prefer, you can make and fill actual bottles.

Try to hold on to all the details, the smells, the sounds, the tastes, the feelings, the movements, and more of each memory and moment...

Activity 31
My Treasure Box Diary

Days of the week and date	Things to ask myself: (draw, collage, record, sculpt, or write) What was a good thing I did today? (What positive qualities does that say about me?) What went well today? What was a positive thing in other people or the world that I saw, noticed, or heard about today? What was my favourite thing about today? (A thing that made me smile, or a moment that I would bottle up if I could?) At what moment today did I feel good about myself, proud of myself, have fun, or laugh?
Monday	
Tuesday	
Wednesday	

Thursday	
Friday	
Saturday	
Sunday	
Other thoughts and things to remember	

Our Very Own Team of Life Cheerleaders, Supporters, and Special Helpers

When Gilly the Giraffe was feeling upset, stuck, or unsure, she had her teacher and lots of her friends to help and support her, like Binnie the Baboon, Loren the Lioness, Oli the Oxpecker, and Wally the Warthog.

We all need a team of people who can help us and cheer us on, because together we are much stronger!

- Who are your special friends, supporters, cheerleaders, and helpers? (These can be real, imagined, celebrities, role models, family, friends, neighbours, teachers, professionals, animals, superheroes, dead people, and so on. It could be people you know really well, or have just met.) In the space below, write down their names. _____

  _____

  _____

  _____

- What kind and caring words have they said or would they say to you? How do you look from their eyes? What do they like, appreciate, admire, love, notice about you? _____

  _____

  _____

  _____

Once you have written down the above names and some of the qualities and words of wisdom, it can be helpful and fun to make a piece of art, such as a drawing, a sand world, or a sculpture, to show to all those who support you.

When you are feeling sad, alone, or worried, you can look at this piece of art and remember you are not alone. You have a whole team around you who believe in you and care about you, and are there for you — people who are in your heart, and in your head.

This also means that whatever worry, problem, or situation you are facing, there is a whole team supporting you and outsmarting the worry, problem, or situation! In a game of tug of war, the 'problem' has no chance!

You can create any piece of art — there is no right or wrong way — but here are some ideas to give you some inspiration! These use paper dolls, collage, miniatures, stickers, sand, a life boat, and a safety net to show people's life cheerleaders, supporters, and helpers.

Photo blanket

Create a photo blanket, pillow, wallpaper, or item of clothing. This can have lots of photos of all of the people in your life who love and support you.

Use fabric pens to draw these people and illustrate the good things they have said to you on a blanket, pillow, canvas, and so on.

Person eco map

Use stickers, shapes, buttons, miniatures, or puppets to show the people around you who are there supporting you and cheering you on.

Put yourself in the middle, and then choose who will be around you and what item, colour, or shape they will be.

Keyring people

Make, design, or draw keyring people, stickers, or badges of the people who are there with you, supporting and caring for you and cheering you on.

Sand art

Choose different colours of sand, salt, or glitter to represent all the special people who support you. For example, someone might decide that their mum is red, and their grandpa is blue.

Fill the jar or container up with those different

coloured sands, to remind you that those people are always with you. You can add things like glitter, pebbles, and flowers to the sand art too.

You can also make sand art keyrings, so that you can carry a reminder of your special people wherever you go.

Life boat

Use a toy life boat and miniatures to show the people who are around you supporting and keeping your life boat afloat. You can also draw or make a life boat using pipe cleaners, lollipop sticks, a cereal box, play-doh — be as creative as you like.

Talk about what anchors you, how you weather the storms, and what is in and on your life vest (for example, what people, things, and tools keep you safe and afloat, what tools you have and use).

Cheerleaders

Draw, paint, or make all of your life cheerleaders. These are the people who are around you, supporting you and cheering you on.

You can also write what sort of things they cheer and tell you, and how it makes you feel when you hear those things.

Safety net

Draw, make, or sculpt all of the people who are holding you up in a safety net, making sure you don't fall and are supported and helped back up if you do fall. These are the people who keep you safe and protected.

Paper dolls

Make or draw paper dolls to represent all the different people who are around you, cheering and supporting you.

Photo collage

Make a collage, poster, or painting of all the people who are around you who love, support, and cheer you on.

Now it is your turn. In the space below, take your answers which you wrote down, and make a piece of art of all of your life cheerleaders, supporters, helpers, and friends.

My special team of cheerleaders and life supporters:

When I Think Mean and Horrible Things about Myself

Sometimes, like Gilly, we can find it difficult to see and appreciate the good things about ourselves, especially if we feel that those things make us different and seem as if we don't fit in, or if other people say mean things about us.

Sometimes we need to look at things in a different way, or from a new angle, like Gilly did putting on new glasses or looking through a magic kaleidoscope. For example, if someone thinks they are stupid, that is going to make them feel bad, sad, and maybe not good enough. They also might be more worried about trying things, or about making mistakes. They also might doubt themselves and think about themselves negatively.

All this may affect how they think, feel, and act. A negative thought is not a fact, it is just a thought, but it can weigh down heavily on people. So, if you have a thought such as, 'I am stupid', ask yourself the questions below (grown-ups will support you with this exercise, and they can use their section at the back of the book to aid these discussions).

- If I was a judge or a lawyer, what evidence is there for and against the thought, 'I am...?'
- How does thinking 'I am...' make me feel? How helpful is it?
- Is there a fairer, kinder, and more positive way of saying this?
- Is there another way I can look at this? How would someone who loves and truly knows me see me?

People Teasing and Saying Mean and Horrible Things

When people say horrible and mean things about us, it can be very upsetting. It can make us feel sad, worried, scared, angry, and lots of other feelings. It is even worse when we hear these things lots, and if we start to believe them. If this happens, there are lots of different things we can do.

We can remind ourselves of all of the things that make us cool, different, and special (Activities 6–25).

We can remember that there are lots of other people who disagree, and who think lots of positive and happy things about us, and that they are cheering us on (Activity 32).

We can think of a reply to say to these people. The grown-up helping you with this activity book can support you to choose an answer that you are happy with; and then you can practise saying it and role-playing it.

We can remember all of the times, moments, and memories that were good, and which make us feel happy, safe, and loved (Activities 27–31).

We can share and talk to people who understand us, who care, and who will help us.

We can learn to do some things to help us cope and relax (see *A Therapeutic Treasure Deck of Grounding, Soothing, Coping, and Regulating Cards* and *Presley the Pug and His Quest for Calm* by Dr. Karen Treisman).

Getting rid of the mean words

We can also write down or draw the mean things someone or people are saying about us on a piece of paper and do the following to get rid of them.

- Put them inside a bottle and watch them float away.
- Put them inside or write them on a balloon that you release; or imagine them floating away on a hot air balloon, or on a soaring magic carpet in the sky.
- Put them inside a rubbish bag and throw them away.
- Burn, rip up, or bury the piece of paper.
- Write the words on a piece of tissue, and watch the words fade away when the tissue is dipped into water, or when the paper is flushed down the toilet.

- Lock the piece of paper away in a safe, a cupboard, or a sealed container.
- Write down the negative words on labels or stickers, and then rip them off, or replace them with positively worded stickers.
- Write the words down on a piece of paper and use scissors to cut them out.
- Write the words down on sand, clay, or on an Etch-A-Sketch; and then remove them, make them fade, or blur them out.

It is helpful with all of these exercises to reflect on and to say out loud how much stronger and bigger you are than the words on the paper.

Changing the situation and mean words

We can also, with the help of an adult, change the situation in our minds. This is called imagery re-scripting. For example, we can imagine, draw, sculpt, or write down the person saying mean and hurtful comments to us:

- with a funny face on
- with a small head or having shrunk to be tiny
- being on mute, paused, fuzzy, or in black and white

- stuck behind a screen, a fence, a tower, a piece of glass, or a wall
- being tiny compared to us who have grown to become a giant.

We can also imagine, draw, sculpt ourselves:

- being surrounded and supported by our team of cheerleaders (Activity 32)
- being protected from the hurtful comments by a special shield, a magic cape, a bullet-proof jacket, a safety bubble, a guardian angel, or a magic blanket.

Suzie being protected from the mean words by being inside a magic safety bubble.

Camden being protected and bouncing the mean words away by wearing his own superhero cape and cuff.

Mohammad being watched over by a kind guardian angel.

Evan turning the person saying mean words into a silly creature, and making them fuzzy and distant behind bubble wrap.

Activity 35
Overcoming Challenges

Draw, sculpt, mould, or write all of the different things which you have overcome, and soon building your confidence and self-belief can be added to this list!

It can be fun to show these things that we have overcome and navigated through by using mountains, an obstacle course, or a maze, for example. *It is also important to think about what skills, strengths, and positive qualities you used to overcome these things – how did you learn these? What do they mean to you? Who appreciates them?*

Showing the journey I have travelled, and the ups and downs, using snakes and ladders.

Showing the challenges and things I have overcome using a maze.

Showing the obstacles I have navigated through by using an obstacle course.

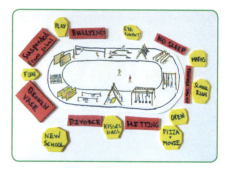

Things I have overcome

My Hopes and Dreams

Write a letter to your future self about what you hope you are doing, being, and feeling. This could be a 'things I want to do' list as well. You might also want to draw, paint, or make a collage of your hopes and dreams. Think big, believe in yourself and reach for the stars!

Write or draw your hopes, dreams, and wishes for yourself, the world, and other people on and around the genie's lamp.

Activity 37
Certificate

Congratulations for having completed these activities — you deserve this award to celebrate your strengths and positive qualities!

Certificate

SHINING STAR AWARD

This certificate is awarded to

. . . .

For being special, cool, unique, and YOU!

Signed: . . . .

Date: . . . .

Gilly the Giraffe

Guide for Adults

Introduction

This book is intended to give you lots of ideas and strategies in order to strengthen children's self-esteem and confidence. The ideas are intended to offer guidance and suggestions; they are not prescriptive or exhaustive in any way. Each child will respond differently, as each of us is unique. After all, that is the whole premise of the book – that we are all different and unique. Feel free to take the ideas and apply them creatively and sensitively to the specific child you are supporting.

Some children will simply enjoy the story of Gilly the Giraffe as a standalone story, and it will be helpful and fun in itself. Some may benefit from trying one or two of the included activities, while others – particularly those who have low self-esteem and self-worth, and it is impacting them on a day-to-day basis, and those who are being bullied, teased, and have experienced abuse – will most likely benefit from doing the majority of the activities, in addition to other supplementary tasks and interventions.

For this reason, some pages in this book have been designed to be photocopiable, so that if you wish, you can select the suitable activities and give them to the child separately, or stapled together to make their own personalised book. This also means that the same activity can be used several times to target different situations or stages.

With this in mind, before you start the activity book, it can be helpful to ask them some questions about Gilly and gain an understanding of their grasp of the story and the more general topics of self-esteem, pride, identity, and confidence. Activity 3 can support you with this. This sets the scene and gives you an initial understanding as to where the child is at, and also helps you to give them reasons as to why you are going through the activity book with them, and why it might be helpful.

In addition, to accommodate the huge range of children and adults who will be reading this book, I have intentionally offered different exercises for each activity.

This, again, is to offer diversity and choice, and to acknowledge the uniqueness of each child. Together, you and the child you are supporting can choose which exercises are the most appealing and relevant to them.

Please note that these ideas and activities should be presented and worked through after the child has read and engaged with the story book of Gilly (some children might need or like to have it read a few times). The activities should ideally be tried when the child is in a thinking and learning space (i.e. not when they are tired, hungry, distracted, or distressed).

This activity book is intended to be used by someone who has a positive and safe relationship with the child, such as a parent, caregiver, therapist, social worker, or residential worker. While it is written by a clinical psychologist, and is therapeutic in nature, it is important to note that it is not a substitute for therapy, or for a formal clinical intervention. Should the need for a formal intervention be indicated, you are advised to seek professional advice. As you read certain activities, you will have a sense whether they are suitable for the child you are supporting, or whether they feel too complex. Only do what you and the child feel comfortable doing.

The structure of the book

GILLY THE GIRAFFE AND ACCOMPANYING ACTIVITIES

Following on from the Gilly the Giraffe story book, there are a series of activities for the child to complete, and to be able to dip into. These range from word searches, to quizzes, to colouring-in exercises, through to activities intended to support children to recognise, magnify, and celebrate their strengths and their positive qualities. These can be completed by the child alone; however, their magic and effectiveness are likely to be much greater if done with a grown-up, and in a positive and trusting relationship.

This section of the book gives you lots of tips, ideas, and games for supporting this process, which is why it is important to read it first.

UNDERSTANDING A BIT MORE ABOUT SELF-ESTEEM

This section starts by explaining a bit about self-esteem and how it can be developed and maintained. This is important, as the more understanding we have of self-esteem, the more we can validate the child's experience and empathise with them, as well as finding some child-friendly words and ways to support them to make sense of it. There are also some sections of boxed text which aim to address some of the common dilemmas faced, for example, 'I have my own experience of and relationship to praise and self-esteem which can impact on how I do the activities, and beyond', 'My child can't accept, hear, or receive praise', or 'My child finds it difficult to identify, or think of any positives'. These are included as they are common obstacles and dilemmas; however, if they are not relevant to you and the child you are supporting, feel free to skip them.

POSITIVE PARENTING IDEAS AND TIPS FOR CREATING
A STRENGTHS-BASED ETHOS AND WAY OF BEING

After the background information on self-esteem, there are ideas and tips for adults to use in actively supporting and strengthening children's self-esteem and confidence. These ideas are integral, and therefore should be read and under-stood first – they provide key components that help to promote an overall positive and strengths-based attitude and ethos, which will make a huge difference to a child's self-esteem.

IDEAS FOR SUPPORTING CHILDREN TO STRENGTHEN
THEIR SELF-ESTEEM AND CONFIDENCE

Following the positive parenting tips, there are some creative activities and ideas for enhancing self-esteem and confidence. These are not prescriptive and are simply ideas that the reader can creatively apply and tailor to the individual child. Some supporting activities are provided, with references to the activities in Parts 1 and 2.

ORDER OF ACTIVITIES AND TASKS

It is important to remember that while this book has been written with an order and sequence in mind, it is not intended to be offered as a step-by-step programme. Some children might skip a bunch of exercises, only do one or two activities, or only find one section helpful, whereas others might find it fun and useful to go through each activity. This is why it is important for the supporting adult to read through this book *first* and to familiarise themselves with it, as well as knowing the individual child. I hope you find these ideas helpful, creative, and fun!

Why are positive self-esteem and confidence so important and protective?

Take a moment to reflect on what self-esteem and confidence look like and mean to you (or even better make it multi-sensory and use all of the different parts of your brain by creating a poster). What words, feelings, images, sensations, and metaphors come to mind when you think about positive and healthy self-esteem and confidence?

Also, reflect on, and if possible visually show, why you think positive self-esteem is important and beneficial. What are some of the hazards and disadvantages if self-esteem and confidence are low? What words, feelings, images, sensations, and metaphors come to mind when you think about negative and poor self-esteem and confidence? This can support the types of discussions you can have with the child about self-esteem, as well as possibly identifying some information about your own position, experiences, and biases around this topic.

Positive self-esteem and confidence are extremely important for everyone! They can have significant ripple effects throughout our lifetimes, and on our overall sense of self. For example, positive self-esteem can affect how a person feels about themselves, what they feel they are worthy of and deserve, including things like love and respect. In addition, it can also influence what they might work towards and strive for, and how they might approach, cope with, and respond to a range of situations, stressors, and circumstances. For example, imagine the difference between a child with high levels of self-esteem and self-belief engaging in a school play, asking another child to be their friend, responding to getting a poor mark in a maths test, making their first job application, or making intimate relationship choices, and a child who feels negatively about themselves and others.

The power of positive self-esteem and positive self-belief should not be under-estimated. In vast amounts of research, it has been shown to be correlated with resilience and other well-being factors, such as positive social behaviour, quality of life, happiness, confidence, and having more effective coping strategies. Therefore, having overall positive self-esteem is likely to be a massive buffer and protective factor for children throughout their lives, and as such, is one of the best qualities we can develop and strengthen in the children we support.

Under this premise, we know that to optimally develop and flourish, children need to feel unconditionally cherished and treasured. They need to have their metaphorical life treasure box filled up, and spilling over with relationship-based memories and life treasures; and to have their treasure box handled with care and treated as precious. This fits with the premise that children need to be delighted and marvelled in; and as Urie Bronfenbrenner[1] aptly says, 'Every child needs at least one adult who is irrationally crazy about him or her.' This also echoes with the saying, 'To the world you are one person, but to one person you are their whole world.' These experiences are essential and support children to develop positive internal voices, and a chain of built-in memories of people who were always unconditionally there for them, consistently believing in them, cheering them on, and supporting them. These can be very protective factors in the face of adversity and life's stressors.

What is low self-esteem?

Everyone at some point struggles with self-doubt, poor confidence, feeling unsure, or comparing themselves negatively with others. This might be in a particular area, such as not feeling confident in one's looks or intelligence; or it might be at a specific time, such as when one is bullied, or has an argument with someone, or has made a mistake. Or it might be on a more generalised level, where the person's overall way of describing and thinking about themselves is negative: 'I'm a horrible person'. Having low self-esteem is a phrase which is often used freely but it is important to keep in mind that all of us make sense of this in different ways, and what one person considers to be healthy self-esteem, another might not, and vice versa. Moreover, esteem needs to be considered within a context, and within multiple layers; for example, someone can have family esteem, community esteem, or cultural esteem.

The phrase having low or poor self-esteem is most commonly used by clinicians when the child's general sense of their self, and their overall opinion of themselves is negative, poor, and critical. These negative opinions, images, beliefs, and self-judgements can impact on their mood, behaviour, descriptions of self, and day-to-day life.

---

1   Bronfenbrenner, U. (2005) *Making Human Beings Human: Bioecological Perspectives on Human Development*. Thousand Oaks, CA: Sage Publications.

Low self-esteem and poor confidence can cover a whole spectrum, and each person is likely to express and experience it differently. There is no one-size-fits-all. However, some common presentations which we see in children with poor self-esteem are shown.

COMMON SIGNS AND INDICATORS TYPICALLY SEEN IN CHILDREN WITH POOR SELF-ESTEEM

- Criticise themselves more and judge themselves more harshly and negatively.
- Use negative words, language, and labels to describe themselves.
- Put themselves down, lack confidence, and doubt their abilities.
- Blame themselves when things go wrong; and/or take an overwhelming responsibility and a harsh stance towards themselves when things go wrong.
- Have high and, at times unrealistic, expectations for themselves.
- Spend a lot of time thinking negatively about themselves and their abilities.
- Focus on their areas of difficulties and perceived weaknesses and flaws, rather than on their strengths and skills. This is like having a negative magnet or superglue, where the negative things stick, and the positive things are repelled, or don't stick.
- Ignore, discount, or minimise the good things about themselves, or about what they do. This can be like having tunnel vision towards the negative, like a negative-focused set of glasses.
- Feel less able, good, skilled, competent, and capable than others; comparing themselves negatively to others.
- Wish they were someone else or that they had a different life (regularly and frequently).
- Feel that their 'ideal self' is significantly different to their perceived 'actual self'.
- Feel embarrassed, disappointed, or ashamed about themselves.
- Are more sensitive to rejection, disapproval, feedback, or criticism.
- Find it more difficult to hear, believe, and absorb praise and positive feedback.
- Avoid or engage less in activities or opportunities where they think they won't be good enough, that they don't deserve to take part in, or where they think they will be judged. They might also assume that they will fail, or that there will be a negative outcome.
- Either take less care of themselves physically and emotionally, or be very focused and zoned-in to being and looking perfect and not making mistakes.
- Assume the worst or focus on bad things that could happen.
- Worry a lot about what other people think, do, and say, and put a lot of weight and focus on their opinions.
- Be shy, cautious, unsure, or passive.
- Be easily led or impressionable, especially if they are trying hard to please others or to get others' approval.
- Feel demotivated and hopeless.

Which of these, if any, apply to the child which you are supporting? Or which, if any, apply to you? Do you have a sense of how these might have developed, or where they might have stemmed from? Do you have a sense of how these might have been triggered, reinforced, and fuelled further?

Why might children struggle with low self-esteem?

Some of the wide-ranging, multi-layered reasons (unique for each child and by no means exhaustive, or in any particular order) as to why children might struggle with their self-esteem and confidence include:

- Having a difference to others which the child perceives negatively, or which receives negative responses from others (e.g. physical appearance, a physical disability, additional learning needs, sexuality, religion, race).
- Having poor life and parenting experiences, such as experiencing domestic violence, neglect, physical abuse, or sexual abuse (see my book *Working with Relational and Developmental Trauma in Children and Adolescents* for a detailed explanation of this). In these contexts, children are more likely to have been exposed to repeated forms of criticism, blame, shame, humiliation, harsh comments, and negative attributions (e.g. 'You're a waste of space', 'You will never amount to anything', 'It's because you're ugly', 'I wish you hadn't been born'), as well as often having experienced being rejected, neglected, ignored, and having their feelings minimised, misunderstood, or ignored. Life and parenting experiences might also include situations such as a parent experiencing symptoms of depression, and the child feeling that it is their fault that their parent is sad, or feeling guilty and self-blaming that they are not able, or good enough to make them feel happy. Another example is where a parent's primary attachment is to substances such as alcohol and drugs, and so the child may feel that they were less important and came secondary to the substance. Or another example is where a child is continually negatively compared to their brother or sister, and where there is clear preferential treatment given on a regular basis to them.
- Being bullied, laughed at, humiliated, picked on, excluded, shamed, and teased. This might be in the context of school, or in other areas by other children and by adults.
- Being in an environment where there was an overall lack of praise, encouragement, and positive acknowledgement, or where there was an overall sense of harsh, critical, and negative comments and behaviour.
- Being aware of negative, judgemental, and critical opinions expressed by others, and behaviours shown by others. This might be individual, but can also relate to wider experiences, such as when there is stigma and discrimination around a family's or community's status, religion, class, race, and so on.
- Having to face a new and unfamiliar situation which may feel overwhelming (e.g. starting a new school, being in a school play, or going for a first sleepover).
- Experiencing wider world pressures and messages such as in the media and on social networking sites (e.g. messages about body image, gender, intelligence, culture).

- Feeling as if they don't fit in, don't belong, and that they are different and often worse than other people (like Gilly felt in the story).
- Feeling pressures, expectations, high standards, and negative comparisons made by others and themselves (e.g. exam pressure).
- Feeling lonely or socially isolated. This includes feeling as if one is not liked or accepted by others.
- Learning negative things from other people (social learning theory), for example, when a child watches other people such as their friends, siblings, parents, and celebrities talk or act negatively about and towards themselves.
- Having certain personality characteristics which make the child possibly more prone to low self-esteem (e.g. being shy, cautious, anxious, self-doubting).

How negative self-esteem can develop and be maintained

These negative self-beliefs and thoughts (e.g. 'I'm stupid', 'I'm ugly', 'I'm not good enough') can develop into something often referred to by practitioners as a core belief or a script. These beliefs inevitably shape and guide the way we see ourselves; and are often the lens and mirror through which we are likely to frame situations, interactions, and experiences. Like a kaleidoscope, it colours how we see things and gives us a unique perspective on how to make sense of things, notice, and respond to them. For example, think about how differently a child may approach making a friend if they think, 'I'm loveable and people like me', compared with if they think, 'I'm boring and rubbish'. Or if a child thinks 'I am stupid', how differently they are likely to feel when they get a low mark on a spelling test.

These beliefs (we all have some) are also often unfortunately given more weight and evidence by life events, experiences, other people's responses, negative labels, and language. For example, if a child already has a strong belief that they are 'stupid', 'ugly', or 'not good enough', and then they hear comments such as, 'He's always rude', 'He'll never change', 'He doesn't want to learn', 'He's just a naughty boy', 'She's such a nightmare', 'She's a trouble-maker', it is likely that these experiences will reinforce and further embed their negative self-beliefs. This is also because most of us are more likely to hold on to the negative information as if it were true, like a highly charged negative  magnet being powered up over and over again; and similarly, we are more likely to discount, ignore, and minimise the positives. For example, if we feel as if we have put on weight, and are looking unattractive, if a whole room tells us how wonderful we look, but one person makes a negative comment about our weight, the majority of us will be more likely to focus on the one negative comment like a magnet, and the other good comments will not stick as much, which can be compared to them falling through a sieve.

These beliefs can also become internalised, and can contribute to a child self-stigmatising, self-blaming, and feeling stuck in a position of learned helplessness (e.g. 'I don't deserve good things', 'I wasn't good enough', 'What is the point in even trying') and so a negative and perpetuating cycle occurs – because of these beliefs, the child often starts to develop rules and assumptions to live by according to this belief (they are often unaware of these rules and assumptions). For instance, a rule might be, 'Because I'm stupid, I must never make mistakes' and an assumption might be, 'I'll never be good enough whatever I do'. This inevitably has a ripple effect and can lead to an unhelpful cycle, involving, for example, not trying new things, spending too much time checking things so that they don't make a mistake that they miss doing other things, or getting so upset and feeling hopeless if they do make a mistake. This negative self-esteem cycle is explained in cognitive behavioural therapy (a type of short-term therapy based on the cognitive and behaviour model) and is shown visually in Figure 2.1.

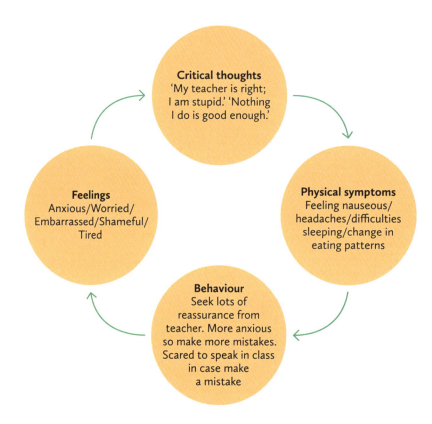

FIGURE 2.1: THE NEGATIVE SELF-ESTEEM CYCLE

In cognitive behavioural therapy, these rules, assumptions, and beliefs are often referred to as thinking/cognitive errors or traps (we all do them at times). Some of these thinking traps are described in the box below. Many of them overlap and interweave with each other. *As you are reading them, think about which ones might apply to you/the child you are supporting.* The more we catch ourselves using them – or support children to catch themselves falling into one of these traps – the more we can understand them, reduce them, find effective solutions, and make fairer assumptions.

Thinking traps

Mental filtering: magnifying the negative and minimising the positive – This is where we pay more attention to certain evidence, usually the negative, and subsequently minimise, ignore, disqualify, or discount the positive. For example, 'My presentation was rubbish' (even though there was an overwhelming positive response); 'Did you see Jacob rolling his eyes and laughing?' (magnifying the one negative). Or, if a child thinks, 'I'm a failure' they might pay attention to all the times that they don't do well in their football game, but discount or minimise the times that they actually do well. They might also put their success down to luck, a fluke, or someone else's actions. If they do well in football, they might say or think, 'It was an easy game'; 'The others didn't try'; 'It was all because of Adam'; or 'It was pure luck'.

All-or-nothing or black and white thinking – For example, 'I'm stupid, so there's no point in even trying'; 'No one likes me; I'll never have any friends'.

Mind-reading – This is where we make an assumption that we know what someone else is thinking or feeling, for example, 'I know no one will like me'; 'She thinks I'm stupid'.

Negative self-labelling and negative self-talk – For example, 'I'm a loser'; 'I'm nothing'; 'I'm pathetic'.

Overgeneralising – This is where a child interprets one event as a generalised pattern. For example, 'I didn't do well in that test; it's because I'm rubbish at school work', or after one argument with one person, saying, 'I don't want to go to school; everyone hates me'.

Catastrophising and focusing on the worst-case scenario – 'Nick didn't talk to me, everyone hates me, I'll never have any friends'; 'I look so ugly; everyone is going to point at me, and laugh'.

Negative comparisons with others – For example, 'She's so much better and prettier than me'; 'Nathan doesn't struggle making friends and playing football; he's so much cooler than me'.

Fortune-telling/future-reading – 'If I join the race, I'll lose, so, there's no point even taking part'; 'I know I won't get picked for the school play'; 'I know I'll embarrass myself tonight'.

As stated above, these thinking traps can be very helpful to explain to children in child-friendly ways; and then to support them to catch themselves when using one of them on a regular basis, and then in addition, to support them to think of a kinder and fairer alternative, verdict, or conclusion.

One of the ways (there are many different ways) in which we can help children to think of kinder and fairer alternatives is to get the child to pretend that they are a lawyer or a judge, and then to support them to investigate, problem-solve, and evaluate the accuracy of the belief or assumption. Activities 33 and 34 and the questions below can also help you to do this with them. These questions might be used to problem-solve and gently challenge these thoughts, rules, and assumptions:

- What negative thoughts did I think today?
- How did they make me feel?
- What am I expecting and assuming will happen?
- What evidence is there for and against thinking that?
- Is this thought or worry based on an actual fact, or on a feeling?
- What conclusions am I making?
- What thinking trap am I falling into? Am I using a negative filter, or jumping to the worst-case scenario?
- How will I cope if the worst-case scenario happens?
- What are the hazards and disadvantages of expecting the worst thing to happen?
- How helpful is holding on to that negative thought?
- What is the best-case scenario?
- What is the most likely thing that will happen?
- Is there any other way I could look at the situation, thought, or worry?
- Would I say that to someone else, like a best friend? What advice would I give a best friend?
- What positive thoughts can I think instead? What would someone who loves or likes me say instead? How do these positive thoughts make me feel?

This introduction has a lot of information to take in about self-esteem. If you would like, it can be helpful to make a visual list or poster of all of the things you have learned, or feel are important when understanding, addressing, and supporting poor confidence and low self-esteem. This might be added to the other poster you did at the beginning of this section, or you could start a different one. You could do a free drawing, or you could have a guiding title like, 'Self-esteem is...', 'Confidence develops by...', 'Key messages about self-esteem are...' This will also help you summarise and consolidate your learning, so that you can think of fun and child-friendly ways to explain this issues to the child you are supporting. This also practises consolidating information visually and is a very helpful activity to do with children after you have had a discussion or taught them something new.

Supporting and strengthening self-esteem and confidence

SOME WAYS TO SUPPORT AND STRENGTHEN SELF-ESTEEM –
TROUBLE-SHOOTING FIRST

We will shortly go on to look at top tips and ideas for positive parenting and creating a strengths-based ethos, followed by some creative activities to do with children to support and strengthen their self-esteem. However, first it feels important to consider our own relationship to praise, encouragement, and self-esteem, as this can have a significant impact on the appropriateness, effectiveness, and delivery of these tools (see the box below). Following this, some further trouble-shooting will be done around children who find it difficult to hear or receive praise and then around children who find it harder to identify positive things about themselves. These feel like important areas to cover first, as they are often the common stumbling blocks parents, caregivers, and professionals encounter when implementing the following activities. If these dilemmas are not relevant to you and the child you are supporting, then please feel free to skip and move on to the next section, which begins by discussing some practical ways of strengthening children's self-esteem.

Our own relationship with praise, encouragement, and positive feedback

The task of giving or receiving praise and encouragement can be further complicated by all of us having our own experiences and relationship with praise, encouragement, positive feedback, and self-esteem. So, it is important to consider the influence of these, before being able to implement the following activities and ideas in a genuine, meaningful, and natural way, or finding a way that fits and feels as comfortable as possible. This is keeping in mind that it can be difficult to model to children the giving and accepting of praise and encouragement if this is not something which we received/receive ourselves. Here are some questions to further explore this area; those who are more visual might want to explore these using a graph, poster, or collage.

- Was praise, encouragement, affection, or positive feedback shown to you as a child? If so, how and in what ways was this given and communicated?
- Who was it given by? When was it given and how often was it given; and what types of things/situations was it given for (try to think of specific examples)?
- What were the messages, sayings, stories, beliefs, values, and actions about praise, self-esteem, self-worth, and positive feedback in your home? These can be across the whole spectrum, for example, 'Too much praise makes children spoilt'; 'Praise should only be reserved for outstanding achievements'; 'I don't want them to get big headed/too big for their boots'; 'Dream big – the world is your oyster'; 'You can achieve anything you set your mind to'; 'In my eyes you're a champion'.
- Did you know when your parents, caregivers, relatives, and teachers were pleased, impressed, and proud of you? If so, how? Can you think of examples of when you were praised, or when you knew you had done something that was positively received?
- How do you think these experiences link to or show themselves in your current relationship to and feelings about praise, positive self-esteem, and self-worth?
- How do you feel physically and emotionally when someone praises you or gives you positive feedback?

- What factors influence your feelings about and responses to praise and positive feedback (try to think of specific examples)?
- How have these been shaped and influenced throughout your life?
- How easy or difficult is it now for you to show, give, and receive praise and positive feedback?
- What factors make giving and receiving praise easier or more difficult?
- What would you like the child you are supporting to learn and feel about praise and confidence? How similar or different would you like this to be to your own experience?

Finding it difficult and/or uncomfortable hearing and receiving praise and positive feedback

Another common apprehension which is often expressed during training and in clinical practice by parents, caregivers, and professionals is around statements such as, 'My child can't accept praise' or 'My child can't think of any positives' or 'Things are so difficult at the moment that I'm finding it hard to like my child'. Therefore, this is briefly explored below, with some ideas offered, while acknowledging the individual differences of each child, parent, and family. Following this, some creative and practical strategies for building strengths, resilience, and self-esteem are presented.

For children who find it difficult or uncomfortable hearing and receiving praise and positive feedback

In addition to grasping the vast cultural, familial, and generational differences around praise and encouragement, it feels important to acknowledge that some children and adults can understandably find it harder than others to hear, and even more so, to believe positive comments, encouragement, and praise. For a variety of reasons, for some people, praise and positive feedback can feel untrue, alien, exposing, fake, conditional, cheesy, awkward, loaded, and so on. In addition, for some children, praise has been associated with trauma and other painful experiences, relationships, and responses.

Everyone is unique and responds differently to different strategies, and unfortunately, there are no magic bullets for getting around this tricky relationship to praise, encouragement, and positive feedback. It often requires large amounts of patience, time, understanding, and creativity. Here are some helpful ideas to begin to address this.

- If appropriate, gently, explore and discuss where the discomfort comes from and how it has developed; reflecting on some of the advantages and hazards of this can be helpful. Metaphors such as the magnet, and the sieve, and positive and negative scales can be used to aid these discussions.
- Use some distancing techniques, such as telling the child what you would like to say if you could, but that you know that you can't because they would

not like it. For example, 'Nelly, I know you don't like compliments, so, I won't say anything, but I wish I could tell you how impressed I was today with your confidence during the class presentation', or 'Ged, I am going to be quiet as I know you told me you can't stand praise, but it's so frustrating because I wish I could tell you about...'

- Share some of the positives about the child with someone else, but while they are within earshot.
- Use non-verbal positive feedback, such as giving a thumbs-up, clapping, giving high fives, or smiling.
- Praise the specific behaviour so that the child knows what they did well, and why they are being praised; for example, there is a difference between saying, 'Good girl' and 'Thanks so much for helping tidy up; that was so kind'.
- Use praise and positive feedback very sparingly, slowly drip feeding it in at key times. In essence, reserve it for genuine occasions, and communicate it in a toned-down way that the child can manage.
- Instead of saying it out loud, or having a face-to-face conversation, write thank-you or appreciative sticky notes, send text messages, or send care parcels (e.g. 'A compliment in the post', 'A hug in a box'), postcards, or letters. These non-face-to-face interactions can also be used when in the car, doing household chores, or when playing a game.
- As adults, we have a huge influence on a child. They are sponges, and are constantly learning, watching, and absorbing what we do, say, and who we are. Therefore, it is important to model behaviour and teach children through our own responses the ability to receive and hear praise and positive feedback.
- Make a positive treasure box, a bottled-up moments item, or a sparkle diary (described below), which the child is aware of but has the choice over if and when they would like to look at it.
- Make a treasure hunt or a hide-and-seek with items game where the child has to look really hard but at each stage discovers a clue or treasure revealing something positive about them.
- Ask the child to support you or teach you something they feel confident in doing (e.g. a computer game, LEGO®, a puzzle).
- Pick up on any positives that they happen to mention in passing, and magnify and discuss these with them. This includes supporting them to positively self-evaluate, for example, 'Wow, that was tough; how did you know how to do that?' or, 'That is very cool; how did you manage that?' or 'What did you do that helped you to get through the day today?'
- Ask the child what ideas they have for how you could let them know when things are going well, or when you have noticed something positive. Support them to think about ways they might feel comfortable with this and want to give it a try. It can also be helpful to reflect on a time they can think of when this happened with someone, and what they liked about it, and also to explore how they show their appreciation to a friend, teacher, toy, and so on. The sentence completion lines in Activity 10 or activities throughout Parts 1 and 2 can support this.

For children who find it harder to identify positives about themselves

- Some children, for various reasons, may not have access to emotional and strengths-based vocabulary (such as happy, embarrassed, and helpful, kind), so they might need some support in first learning and identifying different description words, and exploring what they mean, and what they are like. This might mean going back to basics, but it is a crucial foundation. Activity 8 provides you with a range of strengths-based words which you can use with this. For lots of fun and creative ideas for teaching children about feelings, please see my book *A Therapeutic Treasure Box for Working with Developmental Trauma* (2017).

- Some children may find it easier to practise first by labelling the strengths, skills, and positive qualities of heir friends, families, teachers, toys, puppets, or characters in books or on TV before identifying their own.

- Other children might find it more manageable to discuss positives from a distance, such as talking about them through a story using a third-person narrative (as in Gilly's story) or through role-playing, or using dolls, masks, characters, miniatures, or puppets.

- Talking with children about how you see them through your positive eyes and lens can be helpful (the Take-Back Practice Letter in Activity 40 can be helpful with this). This can also be enhanced by pretending to put on magic glasses, a magic mask, or looking through a kaleidoscope at them.

- It can also be useful to be the child's memory bank and connector. For example, 'Remember the time when you really helped Suzy with her homework? That was so kind and thoughtful' or 'Didn't Mrs Beech give you a sticker for great attendance last Wednesday?' or 'Lisa comes round to visit you a lot and seems to really enjoy it. What do you think she enjoys? What do you think she would miss if she didn't come around?'

- Some children may find it easier to identify some of their positives if they have some form of scaffolding and prompting, such as a ready-made list of positive qualities words which they can circle (see Activity 8) or the adults can use as a guide. Similarly, by having exploratory discussions with the child around topics such as 'If you were to give yourself an award what would it be for?' or 'What good things, memories, moments do you want to stick with you on your positive magnet?' can be helpful (see Activities 24–30, which expand on these questions). In addition, using sentence completion cards can be great in assisting this process, including phrases such as, 'It's a great day when…'; 'I'm happiest when…'; 'The thing that always puts a smile on my face is…' (see Activity 10 or, for a physical game, purchase my resource entitled *A Therapeutic Treasure Deck of Sentence Completion and Feeling Cards*).

- Providing education and information around self-esteem and confidence may also help in supporting children to understand why these conversations may be beneficial, but also why they might find them tricky. Talk about the thinking traps, and support them in exploring which ones they can fall into. You can also use a range of metaphors, such as positive and negative power-up magnets, falling into negative quicksand, filling up a treasure box, getting stuck to a negative thoughts suction, and positive and negative scales.

- It also can be helpful to think with the child about the influence of their perspective, as discussed in the introduction section. These discussions can be supportive in reflecting on how differently we all see and interpret situations, and some of the reasons why this might be the case. Moreover, to illustrate the power of taking multiple perspectives and seeing various angles of a situation (as Gilly the Giraffe did), props such as optical illusions, magic mirrors, magic glasses, and kaleidoscopes can be playfully used. Other ways to demonstrate these concepts (in line with the notion that, like treasures, the more we look for something positive and special, the more we find it) are to hide treats or treasures in a sand tray for the young person to find, to play hidden items games and hide-and-seek games, or to design a treasure hunt for them to take part in. Activity 16 is also useful for this concept.

We have briefly discussed what self-esteem is, how it developed and is maintained, and explored some of the obstacles of carrying out activities around self-esteem. In the next section, some practical strategies are presented for supporting the surrounding adults (e.g. parents, teachers, caregivers, social workers, therapists). As previously stated, these are ways of being and creating a general atmosphere, which ideally should be incorporated into day-to-day life as far as possible. Following this, some fun and creative ways of strengthening children's self-esteem are presented. There will also be accompanying activities for the child to complete alongside an adult; however, the main bulk of activities is in Parts 1 and 2 of this activity book.

Practical strategies, tips, and ways of being for building self-esteem and a positive sense of self

MODELLING POSITIVE SELF-ESTEEM

Surrounding adults should aim to lead by example, teach and model, verbally and non-verbally, self-esteem, pride, and self-confidence. Remember that children are sponges and take in everything that they see and observe. This role-modelling and leading by example might include adults doing self-care practices, such as taking some time out, having a bath, going to the gym, and things like pampering or having little self-treats. This also can include saying self-statements out loud such as, 'I'm really proud of myself today because…', 'I feel really good in this jacket'. It is also important to try to model positive body language, body positioning, and eye contact.

This also includes modelling and making clear to the child that they can try new things, that it is ok and expected to make mistakes. It is crucial that children realise that they can move on from mistakes, and even learn from them. This includes the surrounding adults acknowledging that they have made a mistake and apologising for it.

NAMING, VALIDATING, AND ACKNOWLEDGING A CHILD'S EMOTIONS AND LIVED EXPERIENCES

Crucially, the supporting adults should name, be curious about, interested in, and acknowledge children's feeling and views (the whole spectrum of feelings). This is an essential part of communicating to a child that their feelings matter, are valid, important, accepted, acknowledged, encouraged, and heard. This also includes truly listening, hearing, and taking a deep interest in what they are saying, and in many cases what they are not saying. This listening and validating is also an important step in communicating to the child that they are worthy and lovable, and that they deserve to be loved, listened to, happy, and cared for. (See Chapter 4 in my book *A Therapeutic Treasure Box for Working with Developmental Trauma* (2017) for more discussion and creative ideas on naming, recognising, and acknowledging children's feelings.)

FOCUS ON WHAT WE WANT TO SEE

We need to find ways to communicate to the child what we *want them to do,* and what *behaviours we want to see*, rather, than what we want them to stop doing. This means that, overall, they will be hearing 'do' and 'yes' a lot more (no one is expecting every time; we are only human) than 'stop', 'don't', and 'no'. This means focusing on what you want them to do, so, instead of 'Don't run', you might say, 'Walk by my side or stay close to me', or instead of 'Stop shouting', you might say, 'Speak quietly' or 'Please use your indoor voice'. (See Activity 38 for other examples of alternative phrasing, and for space to try your own statements.)

STRENGTHS-BASED LANGUAGE AND STORYTELLING – LABEL THE BEHAVIOUR, NOT THE CHILD

It is important to hold in mind that language shapes reality, judgement, and our responses. Labels can be so powerful – like tattoos, they can stick throughout a child's journey. Therefore, we would all benefit from consciously and deliberately considering our choice of words, and the way in which we speak to, describe things to, and tell stories to children. For example, if the child is 'misbehaving', we need to try to *label the behaviour, not the child*. This is important, so the child doesn't feel that it is their personality that is fundamentally flawed, or wrong, or that it is them as a person being criticised. This is the difference between saying, 'Naughty boy' (positioning the difficulty within the whole child) and 'It is not ok to hit your sister; hands are not for hitting' (positioning the difficulty within the behaviour, not the child).

REFRAMING LABELS AND DESCRIPTIONS OF CHILDREN

Building on the above notion of the power of language, we also need to try to find ways to positively reframe certain behaviours which aim to position the child in a more positive and less disapproved-of way. For example, although this would be tailored to the unique individual, instead of labelling a child as

'hyperactive', one might say, she is 'energetic' or 'spirited', or instead of describing a child as, 'attention seeking', one might say he is 'attention-needing' or 'attachment seeking' (see Activity 38 for several other examples of positive reframing and suggestions for alternative phrasing).

SHIFT THE FOCUS TO PAY ATTENTION TO POSITIVES

We need to try to have a balance and shift the focus onto emphasising the child's positive strengths, skills, qualities, and resiliencies. This is important as most of us tend to notice the negative more naturally. For instance, how often do we comment when the toilet is not flushed, or the toothpaste lid is left off, but don't acknowledge when the toilet is flushed, or the toothpaste lid is put back on?

Therefore, the more we intentionally look for the positives, and take stock of what the child can do, the more we will appreciate, find, and magnify them. This can be likened to being on an archaeological dig, or on a treasure hunt – the more we look, the more we tend to find and notice things. Along the same lines, think about when you have made a recent purchase, such as a Nissan Micra car. Do you notice how suddenly because you are more aware of that particular car, you see them everywhere, on adverts, on billboards, and on the road? This is because the more we pay attention to something, the more it grows and becomes noticeable!

This is why the more we look for positives in our lives and in our children, the more we will see and notice them. This is a bit like taking our brain to the strengths and positives gym. We need to keep on exercising that part of our brain, so that we are more likely to be able to see and appreciate the positives. The more we see them, the more we will be able to increase, emphasise, and celebrate them, which in turn will push our reward buttons and fill children's emotional tanks and treasure boxes up.

NON-VERBAL AND VERBAL PRAISE AND ENCOURAGEMENT

As discussed previously, some children might respond better to non-verbal expressions of praise, such as giving a thumbs-up, clapping, giving a high-five, or smiling. Where possible, verbal praise should be specific, so that the child knows what the praise is for, and it feels more genuine and purposeful. For example, instead of 'Good boy' or 'Well done', the child might be told, 'Wow, thank you so much for tidying up your toys that is so helpful and kind'. Also, the praise and encouragement should acknowledge effort and trying, not be purely focused on the outcome. For example, 'Goodness, that was tricky. I can see you worked really hard on it', 'Wow, great try, I'm so proud of you for...', or, 'Look how much you have done! You are getting better and better'.

This praise and encouragement also includes supporting them to positively self-evaluate; for example, 'Wow, that was tough; how did you know how to do that?' or 'That is very cool; how did you manage that?'

QUALITY TIME TOGETHER

Ideally, adults should use a variety of relational treasures and experiences on a regular basis to stack the positive side of the child's scale, to power-up their positive magnet, and to fill their treasure box up with positive emotions, memories, and experiences. This gives them lots of happy times to refer to when things are feeling tricky; for example, spending quality time together doing enjoyable activities, and then communicating (verbally and non-verbally) to them about how much you look forward, value, and enjoy this time with them. This can be symbolically, verbally, or creatively added to their positive treasure box or sparkle diary (see the following sections and Activities 27–31). Children also hugely benefit from knowing that they are valued, embraced, and accepted as an individual, and that the people around them really know  them as a unique person (e.g. recognising their likes, dislikes, interests, facial expressions, ways of communicating, triggers). See Activities 12–23 for lots of exercises about getting to know the individual child.

CONFIDENCE-BOOSTING AND CURIOSITY-ENHANCING ACTIVITIES

It can also be helpful to find age-appropriate activities that a child enjoys, and is good at. It is even better if these are confidence-boosting experiences, where they can explore, be curious, adventurous, and playful, and where they can feel a sense of achievement. These can be big or small and will depend on the individual child and their age and abilities; however, they might include things like soft play, messy play, sports, adventure activities, drama, circus skills, finding their way through mazes, conquering an obstacle course, and answering clues on a positive/strengths-themed treasure hunt.

PROVIDING OPPORTUNITIES FOR MASTERY

Find ways to show the child that they can positively affect and influence change, and that their opinion is important, listened to, and valued. This sense of mastery and agency can be worked towards in a variety of ways from day-to-day things like asking what they would like for dinner (or for younger children, giving two choices) and getting them to teach you something that they know about, through to larger involvement in fundraising, social action, and youth-led projects. This can filter down to showing the child that you trust them by giving them some age-appropriate responsibility, such as taking the dog for a walk, or helping with the baking. It can also be useful for children to feel that they have something useful to offer, such as donating old toys to charity, or helping a neighbour who is unwell.

MAXIMISING OPPORTUNITIES FOR SUCCESS

It is important to set up and encourage opportunities where children can experience a feeling of success. A way to support this is by making steps and goals in line with the acronym, SMART (**S**pecific, **M**easurable, **A**chievable, **R**ealistic, and **T**imely) (see Activity 39), in order to maximise the child's opportunities to succeed, have a sense of achievement, and to eventually master the desired skill.

We want children to have a far greater percentage of experiences that go well for them and move them forwards in a positive way, rather than the reverse. For example, if a child is struggling to manage in school and there are several incidents on a daily basis, setting them a goal of having no incidents in a day is likely to be too big an ask, and so each day they are going to feel as if they have not achieved and that it is less likely that they can do it. However, if this started at, for example, an hour, they are more likely to experience it as a stepped approach that is more manageable and have a feeling of success on which they can build and start to develop a feeling of hope and possibility. In addition, to work towards these opportunities of success, we can also support children by anticipating, preparing, and problem-solving potential obstacles.

Drawing, sculpting, moulding, or writing out these obstacles and solutions can make these discussions much more child friendly.

Moreover, the steps taken and distance travelled need to be punctuated, noticed, and celebrated. Some concrete ways of celebrating steps forwards and positive qualities shown are expanded on in the strategies that follow.

KEEPING THE CHILD IN MIND AND SHOWING THEM THAT THEY HAVE BEEN KEPT IN MIND

In line with showing a child they are valued, seen, noticed, and important, where possible show them that you have actively kept them in mind (e.g. have daily check-ins, remember things that they said to you, notice when they are absent, name and label their feelings). This might extend into supporting their sense of belonging through things like having an allocated seat at the table, making a name sign for their door, designing a family crest, or labelling their items.

MAXIMISING ON EVERYDAY ITEMS AND ROUTINES

It can be useful to integrate positive and happy memories and items into everyday routines, for example choosing an uplifting song for their alarm clock sound, eating from their special cereal bowl (which they made, or a special adult made for them), having a diary which they have decorated or contains positive photos, or wearing a positive-themed badge or piece of jewellery. It is also helpful to use daily examples, books, TV programmes, films, and comics to point out examples of being confident, brave, assertive, and so on.

To support the reader to practise some of the above, some accompanying activities now follow, before we go on to explore some more creative and practical activities which can be done directly with children. Please note, as previously mentioned, the majority of the activities are found in Parts 1 and 2.

Positive Reframing and Alternatives to Don't, Stop, and No

State what you do want the child to do. Say what you want, and what behaviours you want to see more of, as opposed to what you don't want to see.

The table below gives some examples of 'No' and 'Don't' statements, and some possible corresponding positive reframes. There are blank rows left at the end for you to add you own individual examples.

Commands and disciplinary statements using don't, stop, and no; and negative descriptors (not prescriptive or exhaustive)	Reframing these to communicate to the child what behaviours we do want to see; and positively reframing the child's behaviours (not prescriptive or exhaustive)
Don't shout	Please speak quietly/Use your indoor voice
Stop running	Please walk beside me/Walk slowly
Don't hit	Please use your kind hands/Keep your hands to yourself
Stop stealing	I need you to leave the items where you found them/Ask before taking something
Don't snatch the toys from...	Share your toys with...
Don't lie	Please tell me the truth
Stop being late	I need you to come home on time
Stop ignoring me	I would really appreciate if you could listen to me/Please use your listening ears
Stop misbehaving	I need you to behave by...
He is so attention seeking	He is attention needing and attachment seeking
She is so resistant	She is understandably cautious and hesitant
He is so hyperactive	He is spirited and energetic
She is manipulative	She has had to learn lots of different ways to get her needs met
He is so easily distracted	He is very easily fascinated, curious, and interested
He doesn't want to try	He must be so exhausted with trying
She refuses to sit still	She seems overstimulated

Activity 39
SMART Goals –Think SMART

SPECIFIC: Be very clear and concrete in what you want to achieve. It needs to be defined. *Ask yourself what specific behaviour do you want to see more of?* Consider breaking the goal down into smaller steps.

For example, instead of 'being good', or 'good behaviour', what specifically do we want to work on or to see? What does 'being good' look like and mean? This might be tweaked to be something more specific, like staying close to me when we go to the park; or brushing your teeth in the morning and at night time.

MEASURABLE: How will you know when you have achieved your goal? How will you be able to measure and monitor this goal/change? What will the child be doing at that time? What will others notice that the child is doing? What will be different? What will the child/you have started, or be doing regularly? What will the child/you have stopped, or be doing less of?

ACHIEVABLE/ATTAINABLE: Ensure that the goals are not too high, or unattainable. Don't set the child and yourself up to fail! Consider setting smaller goals on your way up to the big one. Celebrate your successes. If you don't achieve what you set out to, then ask what you could do differently, what would make it more likely to succeed next time, or to get closer to the goal?

REALISTIC: Is this goal realistic? Are there any measures that need to be put in place to make this more realistic and manageable? Again, think about breaking it down, one step at a time. For example, if a child is struggling to behave in class, and is having several incidents a day in school, is expecting and setting a goal to behave all day or all week realistic? Consider the child's emotional, developmental, and social age and needs versus their chronological age and needs; also, reflect on their journey so far, and the skills which they need to learn first in order to meet the goal.

TIME LIMITED: Set a reasonable and realistic time limit to achieve the goal. When will your goal be re-evaluated/adjusted? When will the behaviour change be measured? When will rewards be given?

Some suggestions for turning a wide goal into something more achievable

If a child/parent/carer says something wide, vague, and non-specific such as, 'I want to be happy', try to break this down into more manageable, achievable, and specific steps. Try to frame the goal, define it, and get a good grasp of what it actually is. It is very difficult to target something, or to make measurable change, if it is so open and large.

For example, what does happiness look like? How will you know you are happy? How will I know you are happy? What would you be doing differently if you were happy? What would be different from now? Talk me through a day-to-day account of what 'doing happiness', or 'being happy' would look like: What things make you feel a bit happy now? Can you describe an example of when you felt happy? What stops you from feeling happy? What makes you feel less happy? How will you know when you are happy enough?

Using scaling questions can also be helpful in narrowing this down. For example, on a scale where 0 is extremely unhappy and things could not get worse, and 10 is extremely happy when things are at the best place where they could be, where would you place yourself? If the child says 3, you might explore what is keeping them at a 3, instead of a 0, 1, or 2; following this you may want to reflect with them about what they think would support them to move to a 5, 6, or 7; and what different numbers felt like, and looked like at different times.

Likewise, if a child lists several different things which they would like to work on all at one go, it is important to prioritise these and to think about which one/s are best to work on first, which ones are interconnected, and which ones can wait. It is far easier to make effective change when focusing on one thing at a time, which may have a ripple effect, rather than getting muddled with lots of different complex avenues.

Obstacles/barriers

Consider, reflect on, and anticipate any obstacles and barriers which may impact the success of achieving the proposed goal (these can helpfully be drawn, sculpted, or described as metaphors). Plan and problem-solve around how these may be reduced, minimised, or managed.

CREATIVE WAYS OF GOAL SETTING

1. Discuss the child's wishes. Props such as a wand, a magic ball, a genie, a dreamcatcher, a fortune teller, a fairy, and an angel can be helpful in bringing this process alive.
2. Support the child to think about what and how they would want things to be different. Using props or metaphors, such as a time machine, a magic door, or a time capsule, can aid these conversations.
3. Pictorially represent different steps and journeys to get to this place, for example by using images of ladders, steps, a path, a road, snakes and ladders, pieces of LEGO®, and/or pieces of a puzzle.

Strengths-Based Approach: Writing a Take-Back Practice Letter

Guidance on how to use these questions

The following questions offer some possibilities and options for reflecting on and identifying the strengths, skills, and positive qualities of children, carers, families, parents, and colleagues. These can be powerfully pulled together and documented in a letter, email, poem, story, or card. Alternatively, these can be recorded on a video camera or phone. They can also draw on responses and input from the team around the child/family. You might prefer just to choose one or two questions to think about, rather than the whole list. Sometimes, you give the person the letter; other times, it is just helpful to shift and open thinking to be more strengths-based and balanced. This list is not prescriptive or exhaustive. Each question can be expanded on by asking thickening questions and embedding them through creative means.

Think about a child/parent/carer/colleague/client:

- What has gone well? What has been achieved so far? What steps have been taken? What can they do already? Think about their journey and the distance already travelled.
- What hobbies and activities does the child engage in, enjoy, and excel in? What makes them sparkle/get excited/feel proud/be happy?
- What skills, strengths, successes, and positive qualities of theirs have you been struck/inspired/impressed by? What are their superpowers and magic gifts?
- If you were writing a review or recommendation about this person, what positive things would you say to others about them?
- If you had to give them an award for something positive, what would it be for?
- If you were stranded on an island with them, what skills of theirs would you appreciate?
- If they became a different person, or life changed as you know it, what would you miss about them?
- If you were no longer with them or seeing them, what parts of their personality would you miss?
- How has knowing them made an impression on you? What have you learned from them?
- What will you take forward from what you have learned from them?
- What are your wishes, hopes, and dreams for them?
- How can these skills, strengths, successes, and positive qualities be recognised, acknowledged, noticed, celebrated, and built on?

Important tips for all strategies – exhaling, expanding, enriching, and embedding

Before we explore some fun and creative ways to notice, expand, and creatively express children's skills, strengths, talents, and attributes, it is important to say that when doing these activities, the magic comes in two ways. First, the activity is done in a positive, safe, fun, interested, and attuned relationship (so that the experience can be internalised); and second, the answers that the child gives are just a platform for further exploration, expansion, and enrichment. I call this technique exhaling, expanding, enriching, and embedding. The four Es make them meaningful and magical, far more so than a piece of paper or a tick-box exercise. Exhaling means slowing down, soaking it in, pausing, and reflecting. Expanding and enriching mean taking the word or concept and really examining it, appreciating it, and finding ways to learn more about it. Last, embedding means finding creative, verbal, sensory, and body-based ways to process, understand, and integrate the word or concept. Some examples follow.

If during one of the discussions and activities in Parts 1 and 2, a child identifies that they are brave, you might go on to discuss times that they have been brave, what brave looks like, means to them, and how they learned to be brave. You might also think about if bravery was an animal, type of weather, item, or object, what would it be? How do they feel when they are brave, and who appreciates and notices when they are brave? Who else do they know who is brave?

You then might want to creatively expand on this, such as in the following example:

Alice regularly showed the skill of being brave, which when explored, she likened to the qualities shown by a lion. So, Alice made a list and a drawing of all of the times she had been brave, strong, and courageous; she was also asked several questions about how these positive qualities developed, and whom she had known in her life who had shown these qualities or taught her them. Alice was also encouraged to tell some stories of these specific times of being brave, and to write them down and place them in a special memory treasure box. Alice was also supported to make and draw her very own lion shield of strength, which was filled with symbolic pictures, patterns, and photos of her showing strength and bravery. Subsequently, stories were shared about lions and bravery and a diary recording all of her 'lion moments' was kept. Alice also made a lion and bravery collage decorated with inspiring images and quotes. In addition, she was supported to make a portable miniature version of this collage in the form of a lion keyring, so, that she could take it with her to school and to other places. This metaphor also became part of the vocabulary of the house and so each time Alice showed bravery and courage she was reminded by her surrounding adults, 'Wow, the lion is in full force today' or 'That sounds a bit scary; we might need some help from your lion part'.

Noticing, celebrating, praising, and expanding on the child's positive skills, strengths, talents, qualities, and attributes

There are a huge amount of different ideas and creative activities, which can seem overwhelming! This said, there are intentionally lots to allow you to find ones which feel right for the child you are supporting, and for you. It is hoped that there is something for everyone, and for those children who are enjoying them, there are plenty of activities to span over a period of time. Take your time going through them, and underline or jot down which ones you feel might fit and be fun or useful to try! Please look through Parts 1 and 2, as in order to avoid repetition, many more ideas and templates are found there.

PRAISE BOARDS, STRENGTHS CARDS, AND CELEBRATION WALLS

Make or design praise boards, positive work portfolios, strengths cards, certificates, and celebration walls which can be regularly added to. These can be for everyone in the house, group, or building. I have seen some schools or homes having things like a Praise Pod, Strengths Sign, Positive Poster, or Celebration Corner. It can be nice to link the skill to the reward, such as the child being a star in their school play, getting to have a star named after them, or having a star-shaped cuddly toy given to them.

SPARKLE DIARY, TREASURE BOX, JOURNEY/JEWEL JAR, AND BOTTLED BRILLIANCE

Strengths can be further acknowledged, magnified, and celebrated by making a superhero moments diary or sparkle diary (see ideas in Activities 25 and 27; and a template for a diary in Activity 31), sticker book, or scrapbook which celebrates the child's progress, positive qualities, happy memories, and special moments. These can be decorated with gems, jewels, glitter, collage, and images and photos of positive-themed aspects of the child's life.

In addition, celebrating the multiple magical moments and taking a purposeful focus on positives can also be worked towards through filling a treasure box up with written and drawn reminders and memorabilia, or a jar with precious stones, which represents the child's positive qualities, progress, and special memories. It can also be fun to fill a jar or container up every day (journey jar) with sticky notes of positive things (alternatively, you can use stickers or drawings instead) and then to find a time to read, and review, the contents (e.g. once a month, on their birthday, on a difficult day, on New Year's Day). See Activities 27–30 for additional information.

I also like the idea of bottling up special moments (e.g. bottled-up moments from Activity 27). This could be by actually filling bottles up and labelling them, or instead drawing the bottles with the associated contents drawn in (see Activity 30 for a template for doing this). One young person really enjoyed this concept, and extended it herself by getting little jars and boxes, which she wrapped up as if they were gifts, and each time she was having a bad day, she could unwrap one, and then she would wrap it again and add a new one.

TOWER OF STRENGTHS, SKYSCRAPER OF STRENGTHS, PATCHWORK OF POSITIVES, SHIELD OF STRENGTHS, BLANKET OF BRAVERY, A PILLOW OF POSITIVES, AND QUILT OF QUALITIES

It can be helpful to find tangible ways to write down, draw, or visually represent together the child or parent's (it can be great if everyone gets involved when done appropriately) many strengths, positive qualities, and skills (in the context of a positive relationship). Use Activities 10 and 11 to support you with this. There are lots of variations that I find useful in supporting children to identify their strengths:

- Writing or drawing a list of all of their different strengths and positive skills.
- Sculpting or making a collage of all of their different strengths and skills. This can be enhanced by having their name in the middle, their photo in the middle, or a title such as, 'I am...', 'I love...because', 'The reason I love...is because...' (see Activities 11 and 12).
- Making a poster, flag, or sign of all of their different strengths and skills (Activities 11 and 12).
- Writing or reflecting on what award, trophy, or certificate a child would get for their different strengths, skills, efforts, achievements, and qualities (Activity 24).
- Writing a story, song, poem, or a rap about their strengths and skills.
- Making a patchwork of positives, either using materials, papers, fabrics, or a floor puzzle (Activities 18 and 25).
- Making a tower of strengths or skyscraper of strengths – the child's strengths are written, represented, and discussed with each brick or block (using LEGO®, building blocks, Jenga®, or pillows). There is something really powerful about visually seeing a tall tower or structure representing one's strengths and skills (Activities 20 and 25).
- Making or decorating a quilt of qualities, a blanket of bravery, or a pillow of positives – a blanket, quilt, pillow, toy, or other such item is either decorated using fabric pens, or decorated with positive and happy images, words, messages, and memories.
- Designing a shield of strengths, where each section of the shield is decorated with things that make the child feel special, strong, and unique. This can be a drawn shield or one made with cardboard and silver foil.

POSITIVE NAME ACRONYM, POSITIVE PORTRAIT, AND MAGIC MIRROR

Another way of expressing and magnifying children's strengths includes making a positive quality list using a name acronym, as Gilly the Giraffe did in the story (see Activity 9 for a range of images and ideas), for example, for *Kate*, *K* – kind, *A* –affectionate, *T* – trustworthy, *E* – enthusiastic. Children can use Activity 9 to support them in creating a positive name acronym, and other fun and creative ways of expressing and exploring their name, such as using items from nature, different materials, pasta shapes. Also, children can use Activity 8 for inspiration for some positive words, and Activity 10 for some strengths-based sentence completion questions. In addition, the child might like to draw a positive self-portrait (Activity 12) or a picture of them as a superhero (Activity 7), or to stick a photograph of themselves on a piece of paper and write or draw all of their positive qualities and adjectives around the picture (Activity 11). Others might like to draw or decorate a mirror with positive words, materials, and images on or surrounding it.

STRENGTHS SNOWFLAKE AND UNIQUE HAND PRINT

It can also be fun to reflect with a child on their uniqueness, and to celebrate their differences and individuality. I often use either snowflakes, shells, or finger/hand prints as examples, as each of these is unique and different in its own way. You can also talk about animals, as in the Gilly story book, since no two patches on a giraffe are the same! Children can then be supported to make their own snowflakes, shells, and finger prints, and write, draw, or make a collage around them of all the things that make them the person that they are (see Activities 15 and 19).

RAINBOW OF RESOURCES, PUZZLE OF POSITIVES, BRILLIANT BEAUTIFUL BODY, POSITIVE RUSSIAN DOLLS, AND STAR OF STRENGTHS

Other extensions of identifying and representing children's strengths and positive qualities include (see Activities 14 and 25 for lots of pictures and examples of these):

- Writing, drawing, or making a collage with the child of all of their strengths, skills, and positive qualities using an image of the rainbow (you can use Activity 22, Rainbow of Resources) or on another thing such as a sun, a flower, or a heart.
- Writing, drawing, or making a collage of all of the child's strengths on different pieces of a puzzle (positive puzzle person), or on different puzzle pieces of a body outline (see Activity 23).
- Writing, drawing, or making a collage of all of the child's strengths on different parts of the body (brilliant beautiful body). This can be done on a body cut-out, a body drawing, or on a doll.
- Writing, drawing, or making a collage of all of the child's strengths on different corners of a star (star of strengths).
- Showing the child's strengths and different parts of their personality on different Russian dolls or puppets, in an All About Me box or collage (Activities 13–14).

STRENGTHS DOODLE BEAR, BLANKET, T-SHIRT, PILLOW, AND SCARF

Other ways of identifying and celebrating strengths include supporting the child to decorate a T-shirt, a doodle bear, a pillow, a blanket, or a scarf using fabric pens, transferred photos, or badges. They can list or draw all of the positive things which they feel about themselves, and which they have in their life. This can also

be contributed to by all the positive things the team around the child has expressed about them. The items can also have positive self-talk statements, affirmations, and inspirational quotes added to them, as well as any special mementos and items.

CHOCOLATE BOX OF POSITIVE QUALITIES, POSITIVE PEARLS, AND STRENGTH SHELLS/STARS

Adults and children can also be supported to label and decorate items, such as shells, stars, stones, chocolates, and hearts, with all of the things which they love, appreciate, and respect about the child. I also find using a clam puppet helpful for talking about identifying children's 'pearls'.

| A chocolate box of positive qualities. | Writing positive qualities down on stars. | Identifying children's pearls and gifts using a clam puppet. |

POSITIVE AFFIRMATIONS

Identify with the child some positive self-mottos and affirmations, for example, 'I'm strong', 'I'm loved', 'Every day I get better at…', 'I deserve to…', 'I did the best I could', 'I can follow my dreams'. To expand on these positive affirmations, sometimes I will ask a child questions such as:

- If you looked up in the sky and there was a feel-good message guaranteed to put a smile on your face written on the clouds, or being led by an airplane, what would it say?
- If you were going to cheerlead for you, what would you say?
- If you opened a fortune cookie, what message would you like to be inside?

For younger children, these positive affirmations and positive self-talk mottos can be made into poems or catchy rhymes. For example, 'I am as strong as could be, like a lion and a tall rooted tree' or, 'I did the best I could, like any special princess would'.

These positive self-mottos can also be written down, drawn, sculpted, or placed in the middle of a collage; they also can be added to other related items such as their treasure box or a patchwork of positives (Activities 17–25). Some children might also like making a positive self-talk shield, superhero cape, badges, labels, or might like to write their mottos on a teddy.

SELF-ESTEEM GAMES AND QUIZZES

Sometimes, children can find it difficult to answer direct questions about what they are good at, so it can be fun to make it into a game with a group of people. There are so many ways to do this, but one is to write down questions and then to assign a colour to each question. To make this more fun you can use different coloured sweets, pipe cleaners, buttons, straws, and so on. Each time the child picks that colour from a bag or box they can then answer the corresponding question. You could also get a plain ball or design your own dice and theme these around self-esteem and confidence questions.

SELF-ESTEEM CALENDAR

A fun way to share about positive qualities is to make a self-esteem calendar, like an advent calendar, and to put a note about a positive quality or a positive reminder in the different days.

STRENGTHS-BASED JEWELLERY

It can also be fun to make or decorate 'strengths'-inspired jewellery. For example, the child can decorate plain wood jewellery by adding a collage of positive and strengths-based words, or they can make a necklace, bracelet, or anklet with each different coloured or shaped bead representing a strength, skill, positive quality, or supportive person. Other children might like to make a charm bracelet, with each charm representing a particular strength, special memory, adversity survived, and so on.

Strengths-focused jewellery with each colour representing a different strength.

Strengths-focused jewellery with fabric pens.

BODY LANGUAGE AND POSITIONING

Confidence and positive self-esteem can also be linked to different body language on the TV, in magazines, and through role-playing body positions and

day-to-day scenarios. I often find it useful to walk in and out of the room playing the same scenario, but using a different body language, tone of voice, and eye contact, and asking the child to comment and reflect on the similarities and differences. It can be useful to have discussions around what confidence and self-esteem look like, feel, sound like, say, and do. It can be fun to look through magazines and newspapers and get children to choose pictures that they feel represent confidence, and to make a collage.

ROLE MODELS, LIFE CHEERLEADERS, AND SUPPORTERS

It feels important to find ways to build and connect with role models, as this can have an extremely positive influence on children. Therefore, it can be useful to ask the child if they have any heroes or role models and if so, who they are and why. Younger children may prefer to think about these concepts using superheroes, fairies, mystical creatures, and magical power.

In identifying these sources of inspiration, children can draw from poems, quotes, films, books, music, and plays. They might, for example, make a positive song playlist, choose a positive song to be their ring tone on their phone, make a collage centred on an inspirational quote, or write out the words to an inspiring song. The influence of these can be expanded on in several ways, and by asking some of the following questions:

- What can you learn from...about life and living? What images, quotes, or mottos come to mind when you think of...?
- What strengths, positive qualities, and skills can you draw, learn, and build on from...?
- What and how did...overcome...?
- How does...show confidence?
- What strengths and skills do you have which are similar to...?

- What advice might...give to you if they were here? What would...be proud or impressed by if they heard about or met you?
- What would you like...to see you doing and achieving?
- Who would you like to be a role model for?

Also, they might like to imagine that a person or people are with them cheering them on and supporting them. This is particularly helpful when a child feels alone, scared, or overwhelmed. See Activity 32 for a range of ideas and examples around this. For example, Kate was feeling very scared about being in her school play, so we helped her to think of all of the people supporting her. This ranged from Elsa from *Frozen*, to the band One Direction, through to her grandma and parents. She was then able to creatively show all these people around her using a collage, miniatures, and a poster, and when she went to do the play she imagined all these people were with her. This gave her much more confidence.

REFLECTING ON PAST CHALLENGES, THE SKILLS THE CHILD HAS OVERCOME, AND THE JOURNEY THEY HAVE TRAVELLED

To support children to feel more confident and ready to face any current or future challenges, it can be powerful to reflect on times when children have overcome something, been brave and strong, felt confident, been successful, and felt proud. Activity 35 is designed to support children to reflect on this. The following questions might be used to expand on this (the wording of the questions must be tailored to the individual):

* What does this mean and say about you?
* What did you learn about yourself?
* How did others respond to you at these times?
* What supported you in getting through these times?
* Where did you learn that skill from (e.g. being brave)?
* What is your relationship to the skill and quality used and the story and history of that skill?
* Who appreciates and knows you have this skill?

Children can also be supported to write a list, story, poem, song, draw a picture, depict in sand, or make a sculpture of, for example, 'A scene which describes a time when I...', 'All of my achievements', 'The good choices I have already made', 'All of the things I have already done', or 'All of the times that I have felt proud'.

Metaphors can be useful for thinking about conquering challenges or travelling on vast journeys, such as climbing over a mountain, navigating a maze, or surviving a storm. These can also be enhanced through inspirational books, films, and documentaries.

HOPES AND DREAMS

It can be useful to have discussions with children about what their hopes and dreams are. This is important for a number of reasons, including giving them a focus, something to aim for, something to look forward to, and hope of things being better or different. Refer to Activity 36 to aid these discussions. You can use props

such as a genie, a wand, a wizard, and a wishing well. You can then expand and enrich the child's answer. For example, if they say they want to be a teacher, you might ask enriching and expanding questions such as:

* Why do you want to be a teacher?
* What would you like to teach?
* Can you think of a time recently when you taught someone something? What was it? How did it make you and them feel?
* Who has been your favourite teacher, and why?

- If you ruled a school, what would it be like? What would the rules be?
- What would your classroom look like?
- If I interviewed your students when you were a teacher, what would you like them to say about you? Can you draw or model yourself as a teacher?

GETTING RID OF MEAN AND HORRIBLE WORDS AND NAMES

As discussed in the introduction, for many children the reason they experience low self-esteem, or that these feelings are reinforced, is due to hearing horrible names and labels, often through bullying, teasing, and mocking. There are endless ways to support children to try to get some distance from mean words and labels, many of which are beyond the remit of this book. However, a few useful ideas are suggested in Activities 33 and 34. Interested readers should see my book *A Therapeutic Treasure Box for Working with Developmental Trauma* (2017) for more ideas and strategies around this.

I hope you find this book helpful, enjoyable, and fun. I wish you luck and positivity in completing it.

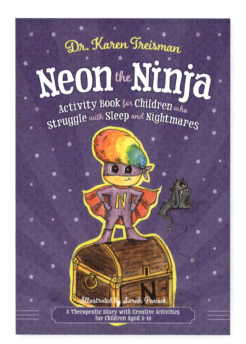

Neon the Ninja Activity Book for Children who Struggle with Sleep and Nightmares

A Therapeutic Story with Creative Activities for Children Aged 5–10

Dr. Karen Treisman

£18.99 | $26.95 | 128PP | PAPERBACK | ISBN: 978 1 78592 550 4 | EISBN: 978 1 78775 002 9

Neon the Ninja has a very special job. He looks after anyone who finds the night time scary. Lots of us have nightmares, but Neon loves nothing more than using his special ninja powers to keep the nightmares and worries far away, and to keep the magical dreams and positive thoughts close by.

It combines a fun illustrated story to show children how Neon the Ninja can reduce their nightmares and night worries with fun activities and therapeutic worksheets to make night times feel safer and more relaxed. This workbook contains a treasure trove of explanations, advice, and practical strategies for parents, carers and professionals. Based on creative, narrative, sensory, and CBT techniques, it is full of tried and tested exercises, tips and techniques to aid and alleviate nightmares and sleeping difficulties. This is a must-have for those working and living with children aged 5–10 who experience nightmares or other sleep-related problems.

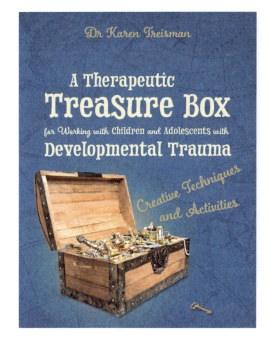

A Therapeutic Treasure Box for Working with Children and Adolescents with Developmental Trauma

Creative Techniques and Activities

Dr. Karen Treisman

£29.99 | $39.95 | 424PP | PAPERBACK | ISBN: 978 1 78592 263 3 | EISBN: 978 1 78450 553 0

Like a treasure chest, this resource overflows with valuable resources – information, ideas and techniques to inspire and support those working with children who have experienced relational and developmental trauma.

Drawing on a range of therapeutic models including systemic, psychodynamic, trauma, sensory, neurobiological, neurocognitive, attachment, cognitive behavioural, and creative ideas, Dr. Karen Treisman explains how we understand trauma and its impact on children, teens, and their families. She details how it can be seen in symptoms such as nightmares, sleeping difficulties, emotional dysregulation, rage, and outbursts.

Theory and strategies are accompanied by a treasure trove of practical, creative, and ready-to-use resources including over 100 illustrated worksheets and handouts, top tips, recommended sample questions, and photographed examples.

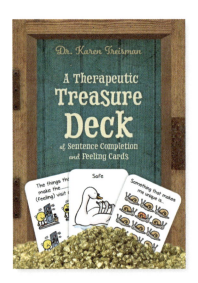

A Therapeutic Treasure Deck of Sentence Completion and Feelings Cards

Dr. Karen Treisman

£22.99 | $29.95 | CARD SET | ISBN: 978 1 78592 398 2

The perfect tool to add to any 'therapeutic treasure box', this set of 68 cards provide a way to help open conversations and structure discussions with children and adolescents aged 6+.

The treasure deck offers a fun, non-threatening way to help to build understanding and forge relationships. It also provides a safe, playful way for children to articulate and make sense of their feelings, thoughts, experiences and beliefs. The deck comes with two different types of card – the 'feelings cards' and the 'sentence-completion cards' – which can be used separately or together, and the cards are accompanied by a booklet which explains some of the different ways in which they can be therapeutically used.

A Therapeutic Treasure Deck of Grounding, Soothing, Coping and Regulating Cards

Dr. Karen Treisman

£22.99 | $32.95 |CARD SET | ISBN: 978 1 78592 529 0

A treasure trove of coping, regulating, grounding, and soothing activities and techniques for working with children (aged 6+), teens and adults.

This pack of 70 cards and explanatory guide offers a playful, non-threatening way to explore feelings, and to form effective coping, regulating, soothing, and grounding strategies through a range of games and activities. Designed to work with both the brain and body, the cards address a wide range of common issues including anxiety, stress, low mood, sleep difficulties and emotional dysregulation. To do so, they employ a range of proven strategies including cognitive techniques, nurturing activities, sensory strategies, body-based activity and creative exercises.